BioCritiques

Bloom's BioCritiques

EDGAR ALLAN POE

Edited and with an introduction by
Harold Bloom
Sterling Professor of the Humanities
Yale University

CHELSEA HOUSE PUBLISHERS
Philadelphia

Library of Congress Cataloging-in-Publication Data

Edgar Allan Poe / edited and with an introduction by Harold Bloom.
　　p. cm. – (Bloom's bio critiques)
　　Includes bibliographical references and index.
　　ISBN 0-7910-6173-6
　　1. Poe, Edgar Allan, 1809-1849—Criticism and interpretation.
　　I. Bloom, Harold. II. Series.
　　PS2638 .E32 2001
　　818'.309—dc21

　　　　　　　　　　　　　　　　2001053901

Chelsea House Publishers
1974 Sproul Road, Suite 400
Broomall, PA 19008-0914

http://www.chelseahouse.com

Contributing editors: Courtney J. Ruffner and Jeff Grieneisen

CONTENTS

User's Guide

These volumes are designed to introduce the reader to the life and work of the world's literary masters. Each volume begins with Harold Bloom's essay "The Work in the Writer" and a volume-specific introduction also written by Professor Bloom. Following these unique introductions is an engaging biography that discusses the major life events and important literary accomplishments of the author under consideration.

Furthermore, each volume includes an original critique that not only traces the themes, symbols, and ideas apparent in the author's works, but strives to put those works into cultural and historical perspectives. In addition to the original critique is a brief selection of significant critical essays previously published on the author and his or her works followed by a concise and informative chronology of the writer's life. Finally, each volume concludes with a bibliography of the writer's works, a list of additional readings, and an index of important themes and ideas.

HAROLD BLOOM

The Work in the Writer

Literary biography found its masterpiece in James Boswell's *Life of Samuel Johnson*. Boswell, when he treated Johnson's writings, implicitly commented upon Johnson as found in his work, even as in the great critic's life. Modern instances of literary biography, such as Richard Ellmann's lives of W. B. Yeats, James Joyce, and Oscar Wilde, essentially follow in Boswell's pattern.

That the writer somehow is in the work, we need not doubt, though with William Shakespeare, writer-of-writers, we almost always need to rely upon pure surmise. The exquisite rancidities of the Problem Plays or Dark Comedies seem to express an extraordinary estrangement of Shakespeare from himself. When we read or attend *Troilus and Cressida* and *Measure for Measure*, we may be startled by particular speeches of Ulysses in the first play, or of Vincentio in the second. These speeches, of Ulysses upon hierarchy or upon time, or of Duke Vincentio upon death, are too strong either for their contexts or for the characters of their speakers. The same phenomenon occurs with Parolles, the military impostor of *All's Well That Ends Well*. Utterly disgraced, he nevertheless affirms: "Simply the thing I am/Shall make me live."

In Shakespeare, more even than in his peers, Dante and Cervantes, meaning always starts itself again through excess or overflow. The strongest of Shakespeare's creatures—Falstaff, Hamlet, Iago, Lear, Cleopatra—have an exuberance that is fiercer than their plays can contain. If Ben Jonson was at all correct in his complaint that "Shakespeare wanted art," it could have been only in a sense that he may not have intended. Where do the personalities of Falstaff or Hamlet touch a limit? What was it in Shakespeare that made the two parts of *Henry IV* and *Hamlet* into "plays unlimited"? Neither Falstaff nor Hamlet will be stopped: their wit, their beautiful, laughing speech, their intensity of being—all these are virtually infinite.

In what ways do Falstaff and Hamlet manifest the writer in the work? Evidently, we can never know, or know enough to answer with any authority. But what would happen if we reversed the question, and asked: How did the work form the writer, Shakespeare?

Of Shakespeare's inwardness, his biography tells us nothing. And yet, to an astonishing extent, Shakespeare created our inwardness. At the least, we can speculate that Shakespeare so lived his life as to conceal the depths of his nature, particularly as he rather prematurely aged. We do not have Shakespeare on Shakespeare, as any good reader of the Sonnets comes to realize: they do not constitute a key that unlocks his heart. No sequence of sonnets could be less confessional or more powerfully detached from the poet's self.

The German poet and universal genius, Goethe, affords a superb contrast to Shakespeare. Of Goethe's life, we know more than everything; I wonder sometimes if we know as much about Napoleon or Freud or any other human being who ever has lived, as we know about Goethe. Everywhere, we can find Goethe in his work, so much so that Goethe seems to crowd the writing out, just as Byron and Oscar Wilde seem to usurp their own literary accomplishments. Goethe, cunning beyond measure, nevertheless invested a rival exuberance in his greatest works that could match his personal charisma. The sublime outrageousness of the Second Part of *Faust*, or of the greater lyric and meditative poems, form a Counter-Sublime to Goethe's own daemonic intensity.

Goethe was fascinated by the daemonic in himself; we can doubt that Shakespeare had any such interests. Evidently, Shakespeare abandoned his acting career just before he composed *Measure for Measure* and *Othello*. I surmise that the egregious interventions by Vincentio and Iago displace the actor's energies into a new kind of mischief-making, a fresh opening to a subtler playwriting-within-the-play.

But what had opened Shakespeare to this new awareness? The answer is the work in the writer, *Hamlet* in Shakespeare. One can go further: it was not so much the play, *Hamlet*, as the character Hamlet, who changed Shakespeare's art forever.

Hamlet's personality is so large and varied that it rivals Goethe's own. Ironically Goethe's Faust, his Hamlet, has no personality at all, and is as colorless as Shakespeare himself seems to have chosen to be. Yet nothing could be more colorful than the Second Part of *Faust*, which is peopled by an astonishing array of monsters, grotesque devils, and classical ghosts.

A contrast between Shakespeare and Goethe demonstrates that in each—but in very different ways—we can better find the work in the person, than we can discover that banal entity, the person in the work. Goethe to many of his contemporaries, seemed to be a mortal god. Shakespeare, so far as we know, seemed an affable, rather ordinary fellow, who aged early and became somewhat withdrawn. Yet Faust, though Mephistopheles battles for his soul, is hardly worth the trouble unless you take him as an idea and not as a person. Hamlet is nearly every-idea-in-one, but he is precisely a personality and a person.

Would Hamlet be so astonishingly persuasive if his father's ghost did not haunt him? Falstaff is more alive than Prince Hal, who says that the devil haunts him in the shape of an old fat man. Three years before composing the final *Hamlet*, Shakespeare invented Falstaff, who then never ceased to haunt his creator. Falstaff and Hamlet may be said to best represent the work in the writer, because their influence upon Shakespeare was prodigious. W.H. Auden accurately observed that Falstaff possesses infinite energy: never tired, never bored, and absolutely both witty and happy until Hal's rejection destroys him. Hamlet too has infinite energy, but in him it is more curse than blessing.

Falstaff and Hamlet can be said to occupy the roles in Shakespeare's invented world that Sancho Panza and Don Quixote possess in Cervantes's. Shakespeare's plays from 1610 on (starting with *Twelfth Night*) are thus analogous to the Second Part of Cervantes's epic novel. Sancho and the Don overtly jostle Cervantes for authorship in the Second Part, even as Cervantes battles against the impostor who has pirated a continuation of his work. As a dramatist, Shakespeare manifests the work in the writer more indirectly. Falstaff's prose genius is revived in the scapegoating of Malvolio by Maria and Sir Toby Belch, while Falstaff's darker insights are developed by Feste's melancholic wit. Hamlet's intellectual resourcefulness, already deadly, becomes poisonous in Iago and in Edmund. Yet we have not crossed into the deeper abysses of the work in the writer in later Shakespeare.

No fictive character, before or since, is Falstaff's equal in self-trust. Sir John, whose delight in himself is contagious, has total confidence both in his self-awareness and in the resources of his language. Hamlet, whose self is as strong, and whose language is as copious, nevertheless distrusts both the self and language. Later Shakespeare is, as it were, much under the influence both of Falstaff and of Hamlet, but they tug him in opposite directions. Shakespeare's own copiousness of language is well-nigh incredible: a vocabulary in excess of twenty-one thousand words, almost eighteen hundred of which he coined himself. And of his word-hoard, nearly half are used only once each, as though the perfect setting for each had been found, and need not be repeated. Love for language and faith in language are Falstaffian attributes. Hamlet will darken both that love and that faith in Shakespeare, and perhaps the Sonnets can best be read as Falstaff and Hamlet counterpointing against one another.

Can we surmise how aware Shakespeare was of Falstaff and Hamlet, once they had played themselves into existence? *Henry IV, Part I* appeared in six quarto editions during Shakespeare's lifetime; *Hamlet* possibly had four. Falstaff and Hamlet were played again and again at the Globe, but Shakespeare knew also that they were being read, and he must have had contact with some of those readers. What would it have been like to discuss Falstaff or Hamlet with one of their early readers (presumably also part of their audience at the Globe), if you were the creator of such demiurges? The question would seem nonsensical to most Shakespeare scholars, but then these days they tend to be either ideologues or moldy figs. How can we recover the uncanniness of Falstaff and of Hamlet, when they now have become so familiar?

A writer's influence upon himself is an unexplored problem in criticism, but such an influence is never free from anxieties. The biocritical problem (which this series attempts to explore) can be divided into two areas, difficult to disengage fully. Accomplished works affect the author's life, and also affect her subsequent writings. It is simpler for me to surmise the effect of *Mrs. Dalloway* and *To the Lighthouse* upon Woolf's late *Between the Acts*, than it is to relate Clarissa Dalloway's suicide and Lily Briscoe's capable endurance in art to the tragic death and complex life of Virginia Woolf.

There are writers whose lives were so vivid that they seem sometimes to obscure the literary achievement: Byron, Wilde, Malraux, Hemingway. But most major Western writers do not live that exuberantly, and the greatest of all, Shakespeare, sometimes appears to have adopted the personal mask of colorlessness. And yet there are heroes of literature who struggled titanically with their own eras—Tolstoy, Milton, Victor Hugo—who nevertheless matter more for their works than their lives.

There are great figures—Emily Dickinson, Wallace Stevens, Willa Cather—who seem to have had so little of the full intensity of life when compared to the vitality of their work, that we might almost speak of the work in the work, rather than even of the work in a person. Emily Brontë might well be the extreme instance of such a visionary, surpassing William Blake in that one regard.

I conclude this general introduction to a series of literary bio-critiques by stating a tentative formula or principle for gauging the many ways in which the work influences the person and her subsequent, later work. Our influence upon ourselves is always related to the Shakespearean invention of self-overhearing, which I have written about in several other contexts. Life, as well as poetry and prose, is overheard rather than simply heard. The writer listens to herself as though she were somebody else, and the will to change begins to operate. The forces that live in us include the prior work we have done, and the dreams and waking visions that evade our dismissals.

HAROLD BLOOM

Introduction

1

Edgar Allan Poe is a perpetual best-seller, even more popular internationally than in the English-speaking world. Poe, in my judgment, was almost always a very bad poet, an inadequate critic, and so dreadful a prose stylist that his tales are improved immensely by translation. Such a judgment is unpopular, because Poe is inescapable. He always will be there, an immense influence upon writers much superior to him, including Dostoevsky and Borges, and all French poets from Baudelaire to Valéry. It is a peculiar irony that Poe is the most widely read American author abroad, surpassing even Mark Twain, Walt Whitman, and William Faulkner.

I published, back in 1984, in *The New York Review of Books*, a review-article on *The Library of America* two-volume edition of Poe. The essay is in print as the Introduction to my first Chelsea House volume, *Edgar Allan Poe: Modern Critical Views* (1985). I remark upon this because of the storm of angry reactions I provoked, including denunciations by the Poe Society over National Public Radio. Poe is something of a sacred cow, and perhaps should be allowed to moo in peace. Certainly, in *this* Introduction, I intend only to be descriptive, as I wish to speculate (with detachment) on the work—tales and poems and *Eureka*—in its possible influence upon the writer, dead of alcoholism at 40.

I recall writing that: "Poe is a great fantasist whose thoughts were commonplace and whose metaphors were dead." Fantasy is a human faculty as well as a literary mode. In Poe, fantasy more often than not manifests itself as nightmare, which is Poe's particular strength. There are a handful of universal authors, who are read (or performed) virtually everywhere, Shakespeare foremost among them. Poe dreamed universal nightmares, and therefore will go on frightening children of all ages, virtually everywhere.

2

Aesthetically, there is not a great deal of difference between typical Poe tales and Vincent Price movies based upon them. Price, an outrageous over-actor, was in his rightful element. As a tale-teller, Poe essentially remains the monologist of his lyric verse, though narrative monologues are an odd form. Ken Frieden usefully observes that Poe transfers the strong presence of the "I" speaking a High Romantic poem (Coleridge, Byron, Shelley) to a still-conversational "I" that tells a story. But the first-person presence in a Poe tale is frequently pathologically a manifestation of the perverse. What was the effect of this monomaniacal narrator upon Poe himself, and his subsequent work?

Poe's major effort was *Eureka: A Prose Poem*, published in 1848, a year before his death. *Eureka* was admirably analyzed by John T. Irwin in his *American Hieroglyphics* (1980) where Poe's turn to cosmology is seen as a last, desperate quest for literary immortality:

> Acknowledging the inherent contradictoriness of man's attempt to represent the origin of the universe in a linguistic discourse, Poe offers *Eureka* to "those who feel rather than to those who think." This split between thought and feeling, mind and body, which the preface of *Eureka* associates with the constitutive opposition between writing self and written self, is, in its ultimately unanalyzable, irreducible character, a microcosm of that opposition between sameness and difference, unity and multiplicity, simplicity and complexity that Poe in his cosmology attempts (unsuccessfully) to reduce to a primal Oneness, the origin and the ultimate destiny of the universe. What the poem *Eureka*, at once pre-Socratic and post-Newtonian, asserts is the truth of the feeling, the bodily intuition, that the diverse objects which the mind discovers in contemplating external nature form a unity, that they are all parts of one body which, if not infinite, is so gigantic as to be beyond both the spatial and temporal limits of human perception. In

Eureka, then, Poe presents us with the paradox of a "unified" macrocosmic body that is without a totalizing image—an alogical, intuitive belief whose "truth" rests upon Poe's sense that cosmologies and myths of origins are forms of internal geography that, under the guise of mapping the physical universe, map the universe of desire. Like the other writers of the American Renaissance, Poe finds himself in the uncertain region between knowledge and belief, waking and dreams, between what compels him intellectually and what moves him emotionally; and like his contemporaries Poe has begun, in the very act of asserting his beliefs, to subordinate those beliefs in crucial and irrevocable ways to his knowledge by allowing that knowledge to dictate the discursive form and logical status of his assertion.

That eloquently gives Poe the best of it, but how does *Eureka* compare to Emerson's *Nature* and his *Essays*, to Melville's *Moby-Dick*, Hawthorne's novels and tales, Thoreau's *Walden*, and Whitman's *Leaves of Grass*? Irwin, I think, is accurate: The great works of the American Renaissance restore a pre-Socratic and High Romantic (post-Newtonian) fusion of rhetoric, psychology, and cosmology. Yet Poe—unlike these five New Englanders and New Yorkers—simply could not achieve the fusion. The same monomania that limits the poems and tales dominates *Eureka*. I quote from very near to the end of this prose-poem:

No thinking being lives who, at some luminous point of his life of thought, has not felt himself lost amid the surges of futile efforts at understanding, or believing, that anything exists *greater than his own soul*. The utter impossibility of any one's soul feeling itself inferior to another; the intense, overwhelming dissatisfaction and rebellion at the thought;—these, with the omniprevalent aspirations at perfection, are but the spiritual, coincident with the material, struggles towards the original Unity—are, to my mind at least, a species of proof far surpassing what Man terms demonstration, that no one soul *is* inferior to another—that nothing is, or can be, superior to any one soul—that each soul is, in part, its own God—its own Creator:—in a word, that God—the material *and* spiritual God—*now* exists solely in the diffused Matter and Spirit of the Universe; and that the regathering of this diffused Matter and Spirit will be but the re-constitution of the *purely Spiritual* and Individual God.

In this view, and this view alone, we comprehend the riddles of Divine Injustice—of Inexorable Fate. In this view alone the existence of Evil becomes intelligible; but in this view it becomes more—it becomes endurable. Our souls no longer rebel at a *Sorrow* which we ourselves have imposed upon ourselves, in furtherance of our own purposes—with a view—if even with a futile view—to the extension of our own *Joy*.

Yet what precisely *is* "this view"? How far are we from the monological narrators of "Ligeia," "William Wilson," "The Black Cat," "The Tell-Tale Heart," and other tales, or from jingles like "Annabel Lee," "The Raven," and "Ulalume"? *Eureka* is an incoherent disaster because it manifests the influence of Poe upon Poe: it could have been written by Roderick Usher himself. Poe indeed is inescapable, despite the plain badness of his writing, and the obscurantism of his thinking. A nightmare monologist can mesmerize multitudes, if he has a genius for nightmares.

KAY CORNELIUS

Biography of Edgar Allan Poe

In a brief life filled with poverty, mental illness, disappointment, and tragedy, Edgar Allan Poe managed to produce a unique body of writing securing his place in the literary canon not only as a poet, and storyteller, but also as an inventor of genres. Poe's accomplishments are even more impressive when weighed against the personal and professional obstacles he faced in achieving them.

Born to struggling actors, an alcoholic father and a long-suffering mother, Poe was orphaned at the age of three and taken in by a financially prosperous family with whom he was constantly at odds. His difficulties with his foster father, in part caused by the man's reticence in financing Poe's early pursuits and in part caused by Poe's own dark personality and penchant for drink, gave him a sense of isolation in this world.

Poe's foster father, in spite of his dislike for Poe, raised him to become a gentleman and succeed in the business world. However, the personality conflicts between the two ensured that this would never happen. Poe's attempts at a formal education at the University of Virginia and at West Point were aborted when his foster father withdrew financial support. He discovered that he was in command of his own destiny, both professionally and financially.

Fortunately, Poe developed a sense of himself as destined for literary greatness at an early age. "With me poetry has not been a purpose but a passion," he wrote in 1845. Unfortunately, afflicted with a financial naivete that would affect his life until the day he died, Poe believed he could make a living selling his creative work. While he published books of his poetry and found critical success in literary magazines, he found out quickly, of course, that sustaining himself was not possible.

Magazines were enjoying a new popularity at the time, and Poe found work editing and writing for magazines. Secure work was especially critical when he married at the age of 27 and took on responsibility for supporting his wife's mother as well. Poe was a dynamic literary critic whose proclamations on several genres of literature affect writers to this day. Unfortunately, he had a tendency to argue with his employers, which, coupled with his alcoholism, caused him to lose many jobs and move around seeking work.

Poe's emotional constitution and life beset by tragedy fostered writing that would earn him a place among the greatest of the Romantic and Gothic writers. Broody and prone to fits of melancholy, Poe had a natural predilection for dramatic themes of lost love and tragic illness. His own wife suffered and eventually died from tuberculosis, providing an icon for many of his works, the sickly, pale beautiful young heroine, immortalized in poems such as "To Helen" and Annabel Lee."

Poe's fascination with the macabre led him to become a master in the horror story. His twist on the genre, influenced no doubt by his own questionable mental fitness, was a protagonist who struggles to prove himself sane, all the while convincing the reader that he is anything but. In stories like "The Tell-Tale Heart," readers soon realize that the first-person narrator who claims to be "nervous—very, very nervous" is, despite his denials, really quite mad. His influence on contemporary horror writers such as Stephen King and Anne Rice is obvious.

In addition to his contribution to horror, Poe was a masterful writer of detective stories. He developed a plot device, which he called "ratiocination", which allowed his hero detectives to solve crimes using deductive logic. In such stories as "The Murders in the Rue Morgue" and "The Purloined Letter," Poe introduced a fictional Parisian detective named C. Auguste Dupin who solved murders and other crimes using clues others overlooked. Sir Arthur Conan Doyle, the famed creator of Sherlock Holmes, called Poe "the father of the detective tale." From the British resident of Baker Street to modern American television's Colombo, fictional detectives who solve crimes by using logic are Dupin's direct descendants.

Other tales by Poe might even be regarded as among the first science fiction. Poe read widely about such subjects as mesmerism (hypnosis) and the hot-air balloon, then the object of much attention. "The Balloon-Hoax," written as if it were a factual news article, tells of a crossing of the Atlantic in only 75 hours by eight men in "Mr. Monck Mason's Flying Machine." After leaving Wales, the balloon is caught in a powerful gale and lands on Sullivan's Island, South Carolina. Another tale, "The Unparalleled Adventures of One Hans Pfaall," also features a hot-air balloon. In it, five years after Hans Pfaall disappears from Rotterdam, a balloon of odd shape and size appears over the city. A strange little person in the balloon drops a letter that describes in pseudo-scientific detail Hans Pfaall's balloon ascension to the moon. Although a concluding note describes this story as a hoax, the balloon stories and others like "A Descent into the Maelstrom" anticipate the subjects of later science fiction stories by Jules Verne and H. G. Wells.

Poe managed to make all these contributions to literature while struggling though an existence filled with misery. He died in 1849 at the age of 40, broke, alcoholic, and perpetually mourning the tragedy of lost love. The irony of his life is that it was these very circumstances that inspired his work, his technical contributions to his craft, and the legacy that remains today.

POE'S CHILDHOOD

Edgar Allan Poe was born in 1809 to a pair of traveling actors, David and Elizabeth Arnold Poe. The lifestyle and financial circumstances of the family were rocky from the start. While theater was extremely popular at the time, actors, with their transient ways and substandard living conditions, were generally regarded as not quite respectable.

Poe's father, David Poe Jr. was born to a highly regarded family in Baltimore. David and Elizabeth Cairnes Poe raised seven children and were respected for their patriotism, hard work, and community service. At the time of the American Revolution, David Poe was a wheelwright who made spinning wheels and weavers' spools. He also ran a dry goods store. In 1779, David Poe Sr. was commissioned as Assistant Quartermaster General for the City of Baltimore. He spent 40,000 silver dollars of his own money to help provide supplies for the Revolutionary War, for which he was never reimbursed. General Lafayette said that David Poe sent him $500 to help feed and clothe his troops and that Mrs. Poe helped to make "with her own hands . . . five hundred pairs of pantaloons."

David Poe wanted his son to become a lawyer, but after taking part in amateur theatricals and founding a thespian club, David Jr. joined a professional troupe in Charleston in 1803. He was a handsome but erratic young man who was only a fair actor and drank to excess.

On the other hand, Elizabeth Arnold—who came from England with her actress mother in 1796—was, by all accounts, beautiful, charming, and an accomplished performer. She first married Charles Hopkins, who died in 1805. She met David Poe Jr. while they were performing together, and they were married, probably in Richmond, Virginia, in the spring of 1806.

The couple continued to travel from one acting engagement to another, even as their family grew to include three children. The oldest, William Henry Leonard Poe, who was known as Henry, was born in Boston on January 30, 1807.

Before their second child was born, Elizabeth Poe was playing the part of Cordelia in *King Lear* in Boston. She decided that if the baby she carried were a girl, she would be named Cordelia. David Poe was acting in the same play, as the bastard villain Edmund. When Elizabeth gave birth to a boy on January 19, 1809, the couple named him Edgar after the character Edmund's legitimate brother.

The last child, a daughter named Rosalie, was born in Norfolk, Virginia, on December 10, 1810. David Poe Jr. was last known to have appeared on stage in October 1809. At this point, his career was ruined by his alcoholism, and he left his family shortly thereafter. He may have died at Norfolk, Virginia, on October 19, 1810, but no proof has yet been found.

By July 1811, Elizabeth Poe was living in Richmond. She had played more than 200 roles in her career as an actress, but now she was struggling to care for herself and her children. The July 26, 1811, issue of the *Norfolk Herald* contains an appeal for funds for Elizabeth Poe: "Left alone, the only support of herself and several small children. . . . Shame on the world that can turn its back on the same person in distress, that it was wont to cherish in prosperity."

Several local matrons answered the call to help the destitute mother, including Mrs. John Allan, childless wife of a prosperous tobacco merchant, and Mrs. William Mackenzie. In spite of their assistance, Elizabeth Poe became ill, probably with pneumonia. She died on December 8, 1811, at the age of 24. After their mother's burial at Old St. John's Church in Richmond, the children were separated. His Baltimore grandparents took in William Poe, while the Mackenzies took Rosalie. Edgar went to the home of Frances and John Allan. They never legally adopted him, but Poe called John Allan "Pa" and Frances Allan "Ma."

At three, Edgar was old enough to remember his mother and to be affected by her final illness. She left him a miniature portrait of herself, on the back of which was written: "For my little son Edgar, who should ever love Boston, the place of his birth, and where his mother found her best, and most sympathetic friends."

From their portraits, Edgar apparently resembled his mother. He is described at that time as a "handsome curly-headed boy" with "big gray eyes." On January 7, 1812, Poe was baptized by the Reverend John Buchanan and christened Edgar Allan Poe. On September 3, 1812, Poe's sister Rosalie was baptized and given the name Rosalie Mackenzie Poe.

In contrast to the succession of shabby boarding houses where Edgar had lived with his mother, the Allans lived in comfortable circumstances in Richmond. When the boy was five, he began his formal education in a "dame school" kept by Clotilda and Elizabeth Fisher. The next year, he moved on to the school of Mr. William Ewing.

In 1815 John Allan's business took him to England, and his wife and Edgar went along. After a visit to his relatives in Scotland, the family settled in London, where they stayed five years. Here Edgar attended a boarding school. Among the subjects he studied were geography, spelling, and the Church of England Catechism. In 1818, he attended the Manor House School at Stoke Newington, also in London. Among the subjects offered was dancing, along with the usual Latin and Greek. In addition, both schools emphasized physical fitness, and Poe became an accomplished athlete.

When John Allan suffered some financial reverses, the family returned to America in July 1820. Edgar returned to school in Richmond. Although many of his schoolmates looked down on him because his birth parents were lowly actors, Edgar's athletic ability brought him some local acclaim. He was able to broad jump more than 21 feet on a dead-level run of 20 yards. In 1824, he swam seven miles up the James River, against a heavy tide. His schoolmaster followed him in a boat in case he needed help, but he completed the swim on his own.

Edgar continued to be an excellent student during his teen years. His best subject was literature, and the English poets Lord Byron and John Keats were his favorite writers. During this time he began to write his first poems. One of his headmasters said of Edgar: "His imaginative powers seemed to take precedence over all other faculties, he gave proof of this in his juvenile compositions; addressed to his young lady friends. He had a sensitive and tender heart."

His "tender heart" led Edgar Poe to feel, with great intensity, the first pangs of unrequited love, which he revealed in an early poem:

> Oh feast my soul, revenge is sweet
> Louisa, take my scorn —
> Curs'd was the hour that saw us meet
> The hour when we were born.

In 1823, when Edgar was 14, one of his school friends, Robert Stanard, took him home to meet his mother, Mrs. Jane Craig Stanard. The beautiful young matron was kind to him, and she became, apart from the vague memory of his own mother, the first of Poe's idealized women. He called her Helen, a name he preferred to the plainer Jane. When he had problems at home or school, he went to her for comfort and advice.

Jane Stanard was dying of a malignant brain tumor. By the spring of 1824 she was bedridden, and Edgar could no longer visit her. Her death on April 28 was a deeply personal loss that plunged him into despair. His friend's mother became the "Helen" in the short poem "To Helen," which many have called Poe's best lyric. (Poe also wrote another, longer poem that was also called "To Helen.") In a tribute filled with classical allusions, he writes:

> Helen, thy beauty, is to me
> Like those Nicean barks of yore,
> That gently, o'er a perfumed sea,
> The weary, way-worn wanderer bore
> To his own native shore.
>
> On desperate seas long wont to roam,
> Thy hyacinth hair, thy classic face,
> Thy Naiad airs, have brought me home
> To the glory that was Greece
> And the grandeur that was Rome,
>
> Lo! in yon brilliant window niche
> How statue-like I see thee stand,
> The agate lamp within thy hand!
> Ah, Psyche, from the regions which
> Are Holy-Land!

In March 1825, John Allan inherited a comfortable fortune from an uncle. In June he bought a large brick mansion called "Moldavia" for $14,950 and moved his family into it. As Allan's heir, Edgar could look forward to a comfortable future. John Allan was a successful businessman and had hoped to train Edgar to work for his firm. But Poe made it clear that he was thoroughly uninterested in business and felt his calling in the realm of literature, which infuriated Allan. The two quarreled constantly.

In 1825, Poe fell in love with Sarah Elmira Royster, and they became secretly engaged. Neither her family, which didn't want their daughter to associate with the son of actors, nor John Allan approved. In part to get his foster son away from Sarah Elmira Royster, but mostly just to get him out of his house—John Allan enrolled Edgar Allan Poe in the University of Virginia.

A Gentleman's Education

Edgar Allan Poe arrived at the University of Virginia on February 14, 1826. John Allan was determined that the university should mold his foster son into a gentleman. Here Poe would establish many of the habits, both academic and self-destructive, that would become the defining patterns of his life.

The university's founder, Thomas Jefferson, wanted Virginia to have "an university on a plan so broad and liberal and modern, as to be worth patronizing with the public support and to be a temptation to the youth of other states to come and drink of the cup of knowledge." The university was a lifelong dream for Jefferson. It was also his culminating achievement, combining as it did his genius as a statesman, political philosopher, and architect. Jefferson built the school in Charlottesville, near his beloved Monticello. He not only designed the school's buildings and distinctive serpentine brick walls; he also set its curriculum, patterned after German universities. Its students were given a traditional education in the classics, enriched by the study of modern languages and contemporary writers, such as Lord Byron. The first term of the school began on March 7, 1825.

Edgar drank from this cup of knowledge, taking honors in Latin and French. He also studied Italian and Spanish and read some history, including a biography of George Washington. Unfortunately, the cup of knowledge wasn't the only cup from which Poe drank. According to the code of the day, a gentleman was expected to drink hard and be able to hold his liquor. Poe joined the sons of Virginia gentlemen in drinking, often to excess. Perhaps for the first time, Edgar Allan Poe discovered that he couldn't "hold his liquor" well—a problem that would plague him through the rest of his life.

Poe also began his lifelong struggles with finances. John Allan, ever frugal, had sent Poe to the university with only $110 with which to pay the annual charges of $350. In addition to drinking, gambling was a favorite pastime at the school, and many business establishments allowed students to run up bills with the assumption that their well-heeled fathers would settle all debts. Poe took to this vice as well. Perhaps in an attempt to increase that money to cover his needs, Poe gambled with what little he had. Predictably, instead of making more money, he soon lost everything, until his debts totaled some $2,000. His foster father refused to pay Poe's "debts of honor." Allan accused Poe of wasting time and money, and Poe complained that his foster father had never given him enough on which to live. He also had financial problems from the very first day.

By December 1826, it was apparent that Poe could not return to the university after the Christmas holiday. As if his other troubles weren't enough, Poe had continued to write letters to Sarah Elmira Royster, his former fiancée. Her father intercepted the letters and urged his daughter to consider the attentions of Alexander Shelton, a wealthy suitor. By the time Edgar Allan Poe returned to Richmond in December, Sarah Elmira was engaged to Shelton.

Back at the Allan's spacious home in Richmond, Poe and his foster father quarreled almost continually, and not only about the debts that Poe felt Allan should have paid. Poe also discovered that Allan had been unfaithful to his wife, Poe's beloved stepmother. Finally, John Allan continued to make slurs about the inferiority of the Poe family in general and Poe's parents in particular.

In 1824, Poe became a lieutenant in the Richmond Junior Volunteers when General Lafayette visited Richmond as part of his tour of America and took part in the ceremonies to welcome the famous Revolutionary War hero. General Lafayette praised David Poe Sr., Edgar Allan Poe's grandfather, and visited his grave, which thrilled Poe and rankled Allan, who'd always looked down upon the entire Poe family.

Finding his home life with John Allan intolerable, Edgar Allan Poe went to Boston, the city of his birth. He wrote his foster father, "My determination is at length taken to leave your house and indeavor (sic) to find some place in this wide world, where I will be treated—not as you have treated me." Now on his own and perhaps determined to show John Allan that his writing would amount to something, Poe spent much of his time trying to find a publisher for *Tamerlane and Other Poems*. He finally persuaded an obscure printer to make up a volume, but perversely signed it "By a Bostonian," as if to ensure that the Richmond Allans would get no credit for his work.

Poe's first published poems feature dream worlds and the long ago and far away. "Tamerlane" is set in a 14th century Middle Eastern country, as a dying warrior recalls his youth. The themes of pride, love, beauty, and death that appear in "Tamerlane" can be found in all of Poe's poetry. In "Dreams," "A Dream," "Stanzas," and "Evening Star," the speaker, as poet, looks to heavenly or imaginary realms for his inspiration. Although not imitations of their work, Poe wrote the poems in the style of popular English poets like Byron and Coleridge.

However, the volume brought the 18-year-old Poe neither the money nor the critical acclaim that he must have hoped for. (Ironically, the few surviving copies now sell for many thousands of dollars.)

Poe lacked training for any particular profession and the means to support himself as the gentleman he envisioned himself to be. Remembering his pleasant days as a Richmond Junior Volunteer and the pride he had in his grandfather Poe's Revolutionary War record, Edgar Allan Poe turned to the military.

Since a gentleman would never serve as an enlisted man, when Poe joined the United States Army on May 27, 1827, he used the name "Edgar A. Perry." Eighteen at the time, the new enlistee claimed to be four years older. Official army documents described him as being five foot eight, with gray eyes, brown hair, and a pale complexion, which pleased Poe who aspired to the Romantic idea of extreme pallor.

Until the beginning of November, Poe lived in the barracks of Fort Independence along Boston Harbor, assigned to Battery H of the First Artillery. Poe's unit was then sent to guard Fort Moultrie on Sullivan's Island, near Charleston, South Carolina. Pirates like Captain Kidd had once used the island and legend said that some of their treasure lay buried somewhere beneath the Spanish moss-draped trees. Poe had never been so far south, and he found the differences in the landscape, plants, and flowers quite striking.

With the help of a local biologist, Dr. Edward Ravenal, Poe learned much about the strange plant, animal, and insect life on the island. In the process of educating himself about his new environment, Poe read widely in the field of natural sciences. He would later use the Sullivan's Island locale for two of his stories, "The Gold-Bug" and "The Balloon-Hoax." However, Poe never wrote about his army experiences, and later would say that he had been traveling in Europe during that time.

On May 1, 1828, Poe was promoted from private soldier to corporal. In December of the same year, his unit was sent to Fort Monroe, Old Point Comfort, Virginia. On January 1, 1829, Edgar A. Perry was promoted to Sergeant Major of the Regiment of Artillery, the highest rank an enlisted man could achieve.

On February 28, 1829, Frances Allan died in Richmond and was buried in the Shockoe Hill Cemetery on March 2. Poe got leave from the army, arriving the evening of March 3. Although the gulf between Poe and his foster father remained deep, Frances Allan's death occasioned a reconciliation of sorts between Poe and his foster father.

Still aspiring to be a "gentleman," Poe set out to pursue an appointment to the United States Military Academy at West Point. Poe admired the colonel in his regiment, and the colonel and Allan both seconded Poe's West Point application.

Poe also had to discharge his obligation as an enlisted man, which he did by "hiring" a Sergeant Graves as a substitute for the rest of his term, which gave Poe a considerable financial obligation. Poe was released from the army on April 15, 1829.

While waiting for his West Point appointment, Poe went to Baltimore, where he acquainted himself with the blood relatives he scarcely knew. Living together were his grandmother Elizabeth Cairnes Poe, David Poe Sr.'s widow; his father's sister, Maria Clemm; his brother Henry; and Maria's little daughter, Virginia. Edgar Allan Poe found he wasn't the only one in his family to have literary aspirations. In 1827, the Baltimore *North American* had published Henry Poe's fictional narrative, "The Pirate." The *North American* also published many poems and a number of other pieces Henry had written.

His brother's success might have encouraged Edgar Allan Poe to try his hand at writing tales as well, but at that time his only interest was finding a publisher for a second volume of his poetry. Using many of the same poems that had been in the first volume, Poe eventually got a Baltimore publisher to print *Al Aaraaf, Tamerlane and Minor Poems*, which appeared in December 1829. John Neal in *Yankee*, a Boston publication, favorably reviewed the poems in this volume in advance of publication. In a letter to Neal that was published as part of the review, Poe declared that poetry was the main purpose of his life.

During this time, John Allan had occasionally sent Poe money, although he refused to underwrite publication of the poems. The second volume of poetry brought no more financial rewards than the first one, and Poe needed money badly. He was still in debt to his army substitute, and in May 1830 he wrote Sergeant Graves to the effect that he could not obtain the money, since "Mr. A. is not often very sober." The sergeant sent the letter on to John Allan, with predictable results.

Allan himself had many concerns on his mind at this time. According to his will, two illegitimate sons were born to him in July 1830, and Allan was courting Louisa Patterson, who became his second wife in October 1830.

In the meantime, the appointment for which Edgar Allan Poe had waited came through, and in June he took the entrance examinations for West Point. He became a cadet the next month. Poe's new friends appreciated his quick wit, and he earned quite a reputation for his satiric verses. Over a hundred of his fellow cadets raised a subscription list in support of the publication of his 1831 volume of poems. Included were the first drafts of some of his greatest poems, such as "To Helen," "Israfel," and "The City in the Sea." He dedicated the book, "To the U.S. Corps of Cadets."

More than 100 years later, in the 1960s, the U.S. Military Academy paid more than $5,000 for a single copy of the book that had sold for $1.25. It is on display in the library's West Point Room, adjacent to a memorial for Poe.

Unfortunately, Poe's West Point experience was cut short. While a cadet at any of the United States' service academies receives a completely free education, including room and board, cadets were expected to produce their own allowance. Apparently still smarting from the Graves episode and eager to wash his hands of his troublesome foster son, Allan refused to send Poe any money.

In a long letter to Allan dated January 3, 1821, Poe wrote, "You sent me to W. Point like a beggar. The same difficulties are threatening me as before at Charlottesville—and I must resign."

However, according to the rules, Poe could not withdraw from West Point without Allan's consent. So, although he had been a very good student until then, Poe decided if Allan would not agree to his resignation, he would allow the academy to expel him. He stopped attending classes and began disregarding orders in January, resulting in a court-martial on February 8, 1831, and his dismissal from the academy on March 6.

With his withdrawal from West Point, Edgar Allan Poe's formal education came to an end. In all, he received an overview of the liberal arts. He had acquired a working knowledge of several foreign languages, which he would put to good use in many of his writings. He was well versed in classical Greek mythology. He had studied rhetoric, the art of speaking and writing. His reading had included some history and a basic knowledge of the natural and physical sciences. Poe's studies in literature had not only given him the tools and devices he used in his own writing, but also equipped him to analyze the work of others.

Yet Edgar Allan Poe's education never really ended. His keen intellect and natural curiosity led him to become a life-long learner. His original ambition to be educated so he could be a "gentleman" had failed. But nothing that he had learned in schools or in the military had been lost. At 21, Edgar Allan Poe stood ready to make his mark on the world.

Editor-in-Chief

After his hasty departure from West Point, Edgar Allan Poe found himself with no place to live. Poe always considered Richmond to be "home," but he had no desire to live in the same city as John Allan. He lived for a time in New York City, but he was unable to find work there. While he still believed he was destined to be a great poet, Poe was realizing that he would need to pursue other literary endeavors to support himself. Baltimore was then an active publishing center, as well as his ancestral home, so he went there.

Poe's grandmother, Elizabeth Cairnes Poe, lived at Mechanics Row on Wilks Street with her daughter, Maria Clemm, and Maria's daughter, Virginia, and Poe's brother Henry. Elizabeth's pension as the widow of a Revolutionary War soldier supported the family. Maria Clemm earned some money repairing clothing. Virginia Clemm, then eight years old, already showed a talent for music. But Poe was to lose another family member when his older brother Henry died on August 1, 1831, presumably from cholera or tuberculosis. He was buried in his grandfather's lot in Westminster Burying Ground.

In Baltimore, Poe worked on his short fiction, hoping to gain the recognition—and income—that his poetry had not yet yielded. From the standpoint of popularity, his switch from poetry to prose was wise. In 19th-century America, magazines were enjoying great popularity. At the same time that people had become better educated, they found themselves with more leisure time for reading. In addition, the improvements in lighting—from candles and smoky oil lamps to much brighter gas light—allowed for comfortable reading at night. For entertainment, reading was a favorite family pastime.

To satisfy the increasing demand for reading matter, general magazines like *The Saturday Evening Post* and women's magazines like *Godey's Lady's Book* published a variety of material. Some magazines came out weekly and others appeared every two weeks or once a month. All sought to fill their pages with information and entertainment that the reading public would purchase.

American writers eagerly submitted their work to these magazines, especially since they had so few other markets. International copyright laws did not exist then, and book publishers often reprinted the poems and novels of popular English writers like Coleridge and Dickens without paying royalties. Forced to compete with this ready source of "free" material, American writers turned to magazines as their best chance for publication.

Writers entered contests sponsored by the magazines in the hope of getting the prize money awarded for the best stories submitted. In response to this opportunity, Poe sent five of his short stories to *The Philadelphia Saturday Courier*—in 1832. He sent "Metzengerstein," "The Duke de l'Omelette," "A Tale of Jerusalem," "A Decided Loss," and "The Bargain Lost." None was considered worthy of the $100 prize for the best story submitted, but *The Philadelphia Saturday Courier* published all five tales—without listing the author's name.

Poe continued to submit stories, only to have them rejected. After a long period in which he had no contact with his foster father, he wrote to Allan in April 1833. The letter was a dramatic appeal for financial support:

> Without friends, without any means, consequently, of obtaining employment, I am perishing—absolutely perishing for want of aid. And yet I am not idle—nor addicted to any vice—nor have I committed any offence against society which would render me deserving of so hard a fate. For God's sake, pity me and save me from destruction.

The letter went unanswered. Thinking he had no other choice, Poe continued writing and hoping to generate an income from his short stories.

In October 1833, Poe entered a competition sponsored by the Baltimore *Saturday Visitor* in which he won a second prize in poetry for "The Coliseum" and the $50 first prize for fiction for "MS Found in a Bottle." The other stories in this batch included "Epimanes," "Lionizing," "The Visionary," "Siope," and "A Descent into the Maelstrom." Of these, "MS Found in a Bottle" and "A Descent into the Maelstrom" show the combination of terror and pseudoscience that would become Poe's trademark.

The contest judges included John Pendleton Kennedy, a novelist and noted literary figure. They announced that they had been impressed with all six of Poe's entries and added that they hoped that all of Mr. Poe's stories would soon be published in book form.

Poe harbored the same desire. By 1833, he had written 11 stories he wanted to put out as a set under the title "Tales From the Folio Club." The format, tales told by members of a fictitious and rather farcical literary club, was similar to Chaucer's *Canterbury Tales* and a later Charles Dickens work about the fictional Pickwick Club. Poe lacked the money to publish them himself, nor could he find anyone willing to do so. However, in 1834, "The Visionary" came out in *Godey's Lady's Book*. It marked the first appearance of Poe's fiction in a magazine with more than local circulation.

Despite the stormy relationship between Edgar Allan Poe and John Allan, Poe must have still harbored some hope that his wealthy foster father would at least remember him in his will. But when John Allan died on March 27, 1834, Poe inherited nothing. He now knew that he could depend on no one but himself for his livelihood, and so far the meager income from his stories and poems wasn't enough to support him.

Magazine journalism seemed to present the best chance for Poe to be paid to work with words. Through the recommendation of John Pendleton Kennedy, one of the judges who had praised his short stories, Poe began in March 1835 to contribute short fiction and book reviews to the *Southern Literary Messenger*, which was published in Richmond. The magazine's owner, Thomas W. White, was looking for someone to help him run the magazine. Poe's lively reviews attracted a wider audience, and soon the circulation of the magazine rose from 500 to 3,500 copies. Poe's salary was $10 a week.

About the time that Poe moved from Baltimore to Richmond in late summer of 1835, his grandmother, Elizabeth Cairnes Poe, died. Without her pension, Maria Clemm was unable to pay the rent and support her daughter Virginia. Hearing of this and unwilling to lose his little family, Poe, then 26, proposed to his 13-year-old cousin Virginia in a letter written August 29, 1835. She accepted, and in October Virginia and Maria Clemm joined Poe in Richmond.

Although a marriage license was issued on September 22, the actual wedding ceremony didn't take place until May 16, 1836. Officiating was the Reverend Amasa Conyers, a Presbyterian minister who was also the editor of the *Southern Religious Telegraph*. Poe called Virginia, "Sis." His pet name for Maria Clemm, who kept the household running, was "Muddie." They both called him "Eddie."

By the end of 1835, Poe had been named editor-in-chief of the *Southern Literary Messenger*. His reviews, in which he waged war on mediocre writing and insisted on high literary standards, were both praised and scorned. In an age that expected literature to be didactic, Poe called such writing "heresy." He urged writers not to form their tastes on what influential British authors were doing. He made his literary judgments independently, without regard for what publishers might think of them. Poe's frank appraisals earned him enemies as well as friends. But while others had written literary criticism before Poe, his insightful reviews made Edgar Allan Poe America's first great critic.

It was a productive time for Poe's own writing, as well. He published some of his previous stories and poems in the magazine and wrote new material, such as "Politian," a verse drama set in Renaissance Italy, and *The Narrative of Arthur Gordon Pym*, Poe's only attempt at a long story. Two installments appeared in the *Messenger*.

Regardless of his stable professional and domestic life, Poe began to suffer from bouts of depression and emotional instability—"melancholy" and "nerves," as he called them. He longed to find something that could offer even a temporary relief from his black moods. Unfortunately, he chose alcohol as his salvation, forgetting his drinking problems in college. By now Poe was an alcoholic. Poe found that one glass was enough to make him lose all sense of dignity and decency. Even worse, he became very quarrelsome when he drank. Writing of his problems with alcohol, he said: "My sensitive temperament could not stand an excitement which was an every-day matter to my companions."

Despite his success as editor of the *Southern Literary Messenger*, the magazine's owner didn't approve of Poe's personal life. Poe's alcoholism was by now interfering with his work. The owner also disliked some of Poe's editorial policies, and in January 1837, White and Poe parted ways. Poe moved to New York, but he failed to find a similar editorial position there. In the summer of 1838, Poe went on to Philadelphia, where he would live for the next five years.

In July 1839 Poe became the editor of *Burton's Gentleman's Magazine*. He also continued, almost frantically, to write more stories and poems. Some of the things Poe turned out during this period can best be called "hack work," either inferior to or greatly unlike the rest of his writing. One such piece is *The Conchologist's First Book*. Professor Thomas Wyatt asked Poe's help in producing a work about seashells, for which Poe wrote the preface and introduction. The book was such a success that it went through three editions by 1845 and became Poe's only book-length commercial success. It also brought an accusation of plagiarism from Captain Thomas Brown, a Scotsman who had published a conchology textbook in 1833.

In addition to several lesser works, Poe also wrote some of his best stories during this time. Works like "Ligeia," "The Fall of the House of Usher," "William Wilson," and "Morella" were published in various magazines, and many readers admired them. But he wasn't as successful with his editorial work. Burton and Poe quarreled over editorial policies, and Poe was fired in the summer of 1840.

Poe attempted to launch his own journal, called *The Penn Magazine*. He put out a prospectus stating that his publication would have "higher literary content" than the popular magazines of the day. A subscription would cost $5.00 a year, with the first issue to be produced in January 1841. However, Poe couldn't obtain the necessary financial support, and the magazine was never published.

While that venture failed, another of Poe's goals was realized when Lea & Blanchard of Philadelphia published 25 of Poe's stories in a two-volume set called *Tales of the Grotesque and Arabesque*. Although Poe never precisely defined the terms, the Arabesques are highly imaginative stories, while the Grotesques have a satirical or burlesque quality. He received the copyright and 20 copies, but nothing else. Poe thought that the publication of these tales would help him to sell his work to periodicals, which were now his sole means of support.

Once again faced with dire poverty, Poe agreed to become the editor of a new publication, *Graham's Magazine*. It became the leading periodical of its day by paying good prices to its contributors, thus attracting quality writing. Under Poe's direction, the magazine's circulation increased from 5,000 to 35,000 copies. In April 1841, Poe published in *Graham's* "The Murders in the Rue Morgue," the first of his tales of "ratiocination," in which a detective solves a crime by logic. Poe also issued a challenge to his readers to send in cryptograms (code puzzles), which he was usually able to solve rather quickly.

Poe's most enduring and important works of literary criticism also came during this time. In discussing Longfellow's *Ballads*, Poe defined poetry as "the Rhythmical Creation of Beauty." In his review of Hawthorne's *Twice-*

Told Tales, Poe established a standard definition and "rules" for the short story, which are still in use today.

Even as Poe wrote his most important work, he was increasingly alarmed at his wife's declining health. One day in January 1842, as she played her piano and sang, Virginia burst a blood vessel. The resulting hemorrhage was the first sign of the tuberculosis that would later claim her life.

On March 6, 1842, the acclaimed English writer Charles Dickens came to Philadelphia on an American tour and asked to be introduced to Edgar Allan Poe. Dickens wanted to meet the American writer who had, in an article for *The Saturday Evening Post*, correctly guessed the ending of Dickens' novel, *Barnaby Rudge*. According to popular custom of the times, Dickens' books were coming out in serial form, one chapter at a time. Readers eagerly awaited each new installment, sometimes even standing in line in front of the magazine offices to be the first to secure the next installment. *Barnaby Rudge* features a great deal of intrigue and an unsolved murder. The title character is a half-wit who has a pet raven named "Grip."

When Poe later used the same kind of bird in his most famous poem, the similarity didn't go unnoticed. In 1848 the American poet James Russell Lowell wrote a tongue-in-cheek review of American writers called "A Fable for Critics." Of Edgar Allan Poe, Lowell says in part, "Here comes Poe with his raven, like Barnaby Rudge/ Three-fifths of him genius and two-fifths sheer fudge.–"

Despite his success at *Graham's*, Poe was dissatisfied with his work and left his editorship in May 1842, apparently this time on good terms with the publisher. He wrote a friend:

> My reason for resigning was disgust with the namby-pamby character of the Magazine—a character which it was impossible to eradicate—I allude to the contemptible pictures, fashion plates, music and love tales. The salary, moreover, did not pay me for the labor I was forced to bestow.

Poe still hoped to found his own magazine, but once more he failed to receive the necessary financial backing. In 1843 he won $100 from Philadelphia's *Dollar Newspaper* for "The Gold-Bug." Flushed with the critical and popular acclaim that greeted that story, Poe published the first of what he hoped would be a series of booklets of reprints of his previous tales. Unfortunately, only one issue, selling for 12.5 cents, was printed. So few copies are still in existence that the Library of Congress has insured its copy of *The Prose Romances of Edgar Allan Poe* for $50,000.

In 1844, Poe moved his family to New York City, which was becoming an increasingly important publishing center. In October he began work on the staff of the *Evening Mirror*. Nathaniel Willis, one of the men who had hired him, later wrote that Poe was a punctual and conscientious employee.

Despite his industry, Poe never left a state of poverty, in spite of efforts to do so. In March 1845, he left the *Mirror* to become one of the editors of the *Broadway Journal*, with the understanding that he would share in the publication's profits, if any. He later took complete control of the *Journal*, which, typically, ran out of money in January 1846.

Poe continued to write criticism and articles for *Godey's Lady's Book* and other periodicals. He also gave lectures and held poetry readings. Poe's most popular poem for performance, "The Raven," first appeared in print in January 1845, when Poe was working at the *Mirror*. It became an immediate success.

"THE RAVEN"

The publication of "The Raven," first in the *Mirror*, and then a month later in the January 29, 1845 issue of *The American Review*, attracted a great deal of attention then, and in the years since its popularity has not diminished. Despite the poem's enthusiastic reception, Poe received only about $15 for the initial printing. The numerous reprints of "The Raven" seldom brought Poe any money, but the poem's wide circulation helped to establish his reputation as a poet. Although many people later claimed to be present when Poe penned "The Raven," he probably wrote it over a period of several months in late 1844, when his wife was seriously ill and they were living in poverty, reflecting his agony at that time.

The phrasing and rhythm of "The Raven" have an almost hypnotic effect on the reader, and its theme of the undying devotion of a lover for his lost "Lenore" has universal appeal. In 1846, when he wrote about the making of the poem in "The Philosophy of Composition," Poe claims "The Raven" to be a carefully constructed intellectual exercise.

Poe began his essay on "The Raven" by declaring his intention to show that his composition of the poem was deliberate, not an accident or the product of intuition. According to Poe, "the work proceeded, step by step, to its completion with the precision and rigid consequence of a mathematical problem." He also denies the idea that his own life, his emotions over the illness and impending death of his wife, influenced his writing. Poe said his intention was to compose a poem that would suit "at once the popular and critical taste."

Having arrived at that intention, Poe's next step was to determine the length of the poem. Since his aim was to create within the reader a degree of excitement that could be sustained, a poem that is too short will fail, as will one that is too long. He decided that a true poem must be short enough to be read all at once, with no more than about 100 lines. At 108 lines, "The Raven," has slightly more. Several of Poe's earliest poems were even longer. According to Poe, " . . . a long poem is, in fact, merely a succession of brief ones—that is to say, of brief poetical effects."

Next, Poe considered the effect that he wanted the poem to have on its readers. "I kept steadily in view the design of rendering the work universally appreciable." To Poe, this meant the contemplation of "the beautiful." He goes on to say:

> Regarding Beauty as my province, my next question referred to the tone of its highest manifestation—and all experience has shown that this tone is one of sadness. Beauty of whatever kind, in its supreme development, invariably excites the sensitive soul to tears. Melancholy is thus the most legitimate of all the poetical tones.

Poe says he looked for "a key-note in the construction of the poem— some pivot on which the whole structure might turn." That pivot, he decided, would be a refrain of only a single word. It would come at the end of each stanza and must fit the melancholy mood, as a word with the "sonorous" sound of the letter "r" would do.

The first word that Poe thought of was "nevermore." He quickly realized that this refrain could never be sensibly spoken by a human being, so Poe settled on having "a raven—a bird of ill-omen—monotonously repeating the one word, "nevermore."

Then, Poe claims, he pondered hypothetically, still not considering his own circumstances. "I asked myself, 'Of all melancholy topics, what according to the universal understanding of mankind, is the most melancholy?' 'Death,' was the obvious reply." Poe went on to reason that the most melancholy death is that associated with beauty and, more specifically, the death of a beautiful woman.

"I now had to combine two ideas, of a lover lamenting his deceased mistress, and a Raven continuously repeating the word 'nevermore,'" Poe explained.

With that idea, the bereft lover would ask a series of questions, with the last "nevermore" involving "the utmost conceivable amount of sorrow and despair." Poe began by writing the last stanza first: "Here then the poem may be said to have its beginning—at the end, where all works of art should begin."

Next, Poe considers his "versification," the meter and rhyme of the poem. Instead of the most common iambic pentameter, having five sets of unaccented and accented syllables per line, "The Raven" uses several combinations of trochaic syllables, in which the accented syllable comes first. (Poe's own name is trochaic — ED-gar AL-lan POE.) The first line of each stanza consists of eight trochaic feet. The second line has just over seven. The third has eight trochaic beats, while the fourth and fifth have seven and a half. The last line of each stanza, the refrain, is the shortest, with only three and a half accented beats to the line. This unusual and original combination was aided, Poe says, by "the application of the principles of rhyme and alliteration."

In addition to having words at the end of lines rhyme, Poe also uses internal rhyme, so in the first line, "dreary" and "weary" rhyme with each other, but "weary," the last word in the line, doesn't rhyme with any other ending word in the stanza.

Alliteration, the repetition of initial consonant sounds, appears in phrases like "weak and weary" and "surcease of sorrow."

Next, Poe says, he had to consider the locale—the place where the lover and the raven would be brought together. He considered, but rejected, the outdoors. A constricted space, he decided, would have "the force of a frame to a picture." He settled upon the man's room (his "chamber"), which would be richly furnished in keeping with the idea of "beauty." Poe then writes:

> The locale being thus determined, I had now to introduce the bird—and the thought of introducing him through the window was inevitable. The idea of making the lover wings of the bird against the shutters, is a 'tapping' at the door, originated in a wish to increase, by prolonging, the reader's curiosity . . . and adopting the half-fancy that it was the spirit of his mistress that knocked.

Poe made the night "tempestuous" to provide a contrast with the serenity of the room and to give the bird a motive for coming inside.

The bird alights on a marble bust of Pallas (Pallas Athena, the Greek goddess of wisdom) for three reasons. First, Poe says, it was white, in contrast with the bird's dark feathers. Second, Pallas was chosen to fit with the implied scholarship of the man, with his "many volumes of forgotten lore." Finally, Poe liked the sound of the word "Pallas."

Poe goes on to recount examples of word choices that would contribute to the desired effects. He writes, ". . . an air of the fantastic—approaching as nearly to the ludicrous as was admissible—is given to the raven's entrance. He comes in with 'many a flirt and flutter' and has 'the mien' (bearing or appearance) of lord or lady."

Unlike poetry in general and many of Poe's previous poems in particular, "The Raven" contains few metaphors. Not until the final stanza, with the words "from out of my heart" does the poet make an implied comparison. "The reader begins now to regard the raven as emblematical . . ."

The poem ends with the poet's realization that, just as the bird's beak will never be lifted from the man's heart, so his soul will never recover from its grief for the lost Lenore.

"The Raven" doesn't end happily, but for Edgar Allan Poe, such a forced outcome was the trademark of commercial fiction and ruined good literature.

Poe's "Philosophy of Composition" also deals with the writing of his tales. In both, he expresses ideas that grew out of his own life, the times in which he lived, and the literary movements that influenced him. For that reason, an examination of Poe's life and work must include a look at Romanticism, the source of many of the writer's ideas about beauty and death.

The Making of a Romantic

The Romantic qualities of Edgar Allan Poe's writing link him to the literary movement that began in Europe and Great Britain in the 18th century and spread to the United States. Romanticism grew out of a revolt against the tradition of neoclassicism, in which reason, form, order, and proportion were of greatest importance. As a result, change came to all the fine arts. Music, painting, sculpture, and literature all became looser in form and more original in thought. Emotion, ranging from shallow sentiment to deep feeling, became more important than reason. Anything original was valued above set forms. Death and the sadness of the bereaved became favorite subjects. Nature assumed great importance, especially since it was "picturesque," and the past, particularly the Medieval period, seemed a far better time than the present. Additionally, Poe's work became classically Gothic, with its themes of mystery and horror.

"The Pleasures of Melancholy," a 1747 work by the English poet Thomas Warton, reflects so many of the Romantic elements that appear in

Poe's writing that Edgar Allan Poe could almost be mistaken as its author. Here is part of that poem, which is written in iambic pentameter:

> Beneath yon ruined abbey's moss-grown piles
> Oft let me sit, at twilight hour of eve,
> Where through some western window the pale moon
> Pours her long-levelled rule of streaming light,
> While sullen, sacred silence reigns around,
> Save the lone screech-owl's note, who builds his bower
> Amid the moldering caverns dark and damp,
> Or the calm breeze that rustles in the leaves
> Of flaunting ivy, that with mantle green
> Invests some wasted tower
>
> But when the world
> Is clad in midnight's raven-colored robe,
> 'Mid hollow charnel let me watch the flame
> Of taper dim, shedding a livid glare
> O'er the wan heaps, while airy voices talk
> Among the glimmering walls, or ghostly shape,
> At distance seen, invites with beckoning hand
> My lonesome steps through the far-winding vaults.
> Nor undelightful is the solemn noon
> Of night, when haply wakeful from my couch
> I start: lo, all is motionless around!
> Roars not the rushing wind; the sons of men
> And every beast in mute oblivion lie;
> All nature's hushed in silence and in sleep:
> O then how fearful is it to reflect
> That through the still globe's awful solitude
> No being wakes but me! till stealing sleep
> My drooping temples bathes in opiate dews,
> Nor then let dreams, of wanton folly born,
> My senses lead through flowery paths of joy . . .

Poe was certainly well-acquainted with the work of the leading English Romantic poets: Lord Byron, Samuel Taylor Coleridge, Percy Bysshe Shelley, John Keats, and William Wordsworth, identifying himself most personally with Byron and Shelley. Each of those Romantics probably contributed something to the shaping of Poe's own unique style.

Lord Byron was born in 1788 and died in 1824, when Edgar Allan Poe was in school in England. Byron looked every inch a poet, with "sable curls in wild profusion" swept back from a high brow above dark, liquid, brooding eyes. His loose, open collar perfectly framed his handsome features. Although he walked with a limp, Byron was an excellent swimmer, and his feat of swimming the Hellespont (the strait between Greece and Turkey) no doubt inspired a young Edgar Allan Poe to imitation when he made his similar swim in the James River. Described as "a man of loneliness and mystery," Byron was cynical and scorned convention, yet he was capable of both passion and remorse. In many ways, Byron and Poe seem similar.

Another English Romantic whom Poe admired was Samuel Taylor Coleridge (1772-1834). Although plagued by intense headaches and the effects of the opiates he took to relive the pain, Coleridge managed to produce important poems of his own, as well as to write about the work of others. Coleridge's essays on Wordsworth's *Lyrical Ballads* greatly influenced Poe's thoughts about poetry and the form of his literary criticism. Among the topics of the Coleridge essays are "Imagination and Fancy," "The Language of Poetry" and "Consequences of the Use of Meter."

Percy Bysshe Shelley (1792-1822) had the most flamboyant personal life of the Romantic poets. He deserted his wife and two children to run away to Europe with Mary Godwin (who would then write *Frankenstein* to prove that a woman could produce a Gothic tale as well as any man). They were married after his first wife's suicide, but when the courts refused to give Shelley custody of his children, he again left England. He was only 30 when he drowned in a sailing accident. His greatest influence on Poe was probably in the sound effects of his verse, which has the same kind of rhapsodic quality of melody utilized by Poe.

John Keats (1795-1821) had the briefest life, and his was also one of the most tragic. His first poetry met savage critical reviews, but he kept writing, even after contracting tuberculosis while nursing his ill brother. Kept from marrying the woman he loved, Keats went to Rome in the hope that a warmer climate would restore his health. Instead, he died there at the age of 26. The worship of beauty was both the motivation and the message of Keats' poetry. One of his poems begins, "A thing of beauty is a joy forever," and his "Ode on a Grecian Urn" ends with the words "Beauty is truth, truth beauty, that is all ye know on earth, and all ye need to know."

William Worsdworth (1770-1850), the great nature poet, was orphaned at the age of three and brought up by an uncle. He resisted the plans made for him to become a doctor and ran away to France, barely escaping with his life when the revolution began. Settling down in the Lake Country of England, he turned to his life's work as a poet. The publication, with Coleridge, of *Lyrical Ballads* is generally regarded as the official doctrine of the English Romantic Movement. In it, the poets sought to explain the Romantics' ideas about returning to nature, glorifying the common man, and dwelling on the supernatural and strange. Wordsworth's best poetry is also his shortest, a fact which Poe seems to have taken to heart.

Poe's writing embodied all the basic characteristics of Romantic writing. To a Romantic, midnight was the most interesting hour, and fall and winter were the best seasons. A landscape that featured a "ruined tower" or grotesquely twisted trees was deemed more desirable than a patterned classical garden. A storm was preferred to calm weather, unless it was the ominous calm foretelling a rattling thunderstorm. For interior settings, rooms should preferably be in a gloomy castle with walls covered by dark, heavy draperies. Dungeons and tower rooms were standard features, along with ghosts and wraiths.

Poe's claim of the death of a beautiful woman as the most suitable subject for poetry is Romantic to the core. But in Poe's case, it seems to be more than a deliberate literary device designed to affect the reader's emotions. The deaths at an early age of both his mother and wife probably served as the inspiration for much of Poe's writing, as well as reinforcing this Romantic belief.

But the author of "The Raven" was far more than a craftsman whose poetry could create certain effects in his readers. Poe was also fascinated with the human mind and went past mere Romantic conventions in both his poetry and his tales.

Poe's artistry is given free rein as his stories explore his main subjects, the way the human mind works and how it reacts to beauty, fear, death, and grief.

It was in his review of Nathaniel Hawthorne's *Twice-Told Tales* in the May 1842 issue of *Graham's Magazine* that Edgar Allan Poe first presented his "rules" for a good tale. Like Poe, Hawthorne had once been a magazine editor, but he withdrew for more than a decade to work on his writing. The first edition of his *Twice-Told Tales* contained 37 stories, including "The Minister's Black Veil," "Dr. Heidigger's Experiment" and "Wakefield." Hawthorne said he wrote best if he gave his narratives "a certain remoteness" from actuality by setting them in the past, in scenes removed from ordinary experience. He also created characters to which he could attach symbolic or allegorical meanings. "In all my stories, I think," Hawthorne wrote, "there is one idea running through them like an iron rod." The resulting story would then have one theme and one message.

Edgar Allan Poe named this quality "unity of effect" and called it a point of "the greatest importance." To achieve this unity, a piece of writing had to be short. As we have seen, Poe limited "The Raven" to around 100 lines for that reason. His guideline for the "prose tale" was similar: the length of the work should allow it to be read in a single sitting. To Poe, this meant it should take a reader between a half-hour and two hours to finish a story.

Poe's second rule for the short story goes along with a story's length. To be brief, a narrative must take place in a fairly restricted space. Characters do not have to be kept in one room all the time—as in Aristotle's rule, "unity of time and place"—but they should not stray far from one central location.

The third requirement for a prose narrative is similar to Aristotle's rule calling for "unity of action." All the details of the narrative must work together as a whole, and everything that is needed to understand a story must be included in it.

Poe achieved his stated goals for the short story in his own writing by using a first-person narrator. All the tales are told by the hero or, in some cases, someone else who relates, in the first person, events that happened to someone else. The use of the first person lends an air of immediacy and reality that the third person never could.

Poe also admired verisimilitude. Literally, the word means "truth-like." As fantastic and grotesque as some of Poe's tales are, the very precision of the details he chooses to include in them lend an air of credibility.

In praising Hawthorne's *Twice-Told Tales*, Poe named the qualities that he felt made them great. "Mr. Hawthorne's distinctive trait is invention, creation, imagination, originality—a trait which, in the literature of fiction, is positively worth all the rest. . . . Mr. Hawthorne is original at all points."

Given his natural tendency toward spells of melancholy and his admiration for all the trappings of Romanticism, particularly of the Gothic novels, Poe was naturally drawn to write "tales of the grotesque and arabesque." Poe also wrote most of his stories with a view to the money they would bring. He shrewdly analyzed the popular fiction being published and understood that readers liked to be taken out of themselves and their ordinary lives. He knew that people liked the vicarious thrills that come from reading tales of horror while being quite safe from direct experience with the unspeakable. Poe judged his audience well. These tales became his best known and most widely read stories. Yet, as much as he needed the money from these tales, Poe remained true to his own literary standards. Considering the types of story others were writing at that time, Poe's tales are remarkably free from hackneyed devices like ghosts, vampires, and werewolves. Instead, his heroes are usually exceptionally well-educated men who struggle with their sanity and the loss of their beautiful, ethereal women.

Although Poe uses a persona (an adopted character other than his real identity) in these stories, the reader with knowledge about the writer's life can see a definite connection between Poe's life and his fiction. As far as is known, at least, Edgar Allan Poe never killed anyone. But during the frequent periods of estrangement with John Allan, Poe might well have imagined killing him, just as the unnamed narrator of "The Tell-Tale Heart" killed an old man whose eye disturbed him. But Poe knew he couldn't get away with such a deed in real life, so the character in the story cannot escape his own conscience.

Entombment and being buried alive are familiar themes in Poe's stories. In "The Cask of Amontillado," Montresor lures Fortunato to his wine cellar, where he walls him up as an act of revenge over some unnamed injuries.

Revenge is also the motive in "Hop-Frog," one of Poe's most graphic tales of horror. In it, a deformed court jester who has endured much torment from the courtiers manages, in the guise of entertaining them, to burn them alive.

In those last two stories, the victims are intoxicated when they meet their fate. In the careful way Poe constructed the stories, it was necessary for the characters not to notice what was happening to them until it was too late.

In other stories, Poe's narrators appear intoxicated, as if the events that they are about to relate are the product of a "fevered brain" or some kind of strange waking nightmare. Poe's heroes also often bear a strong resemblance to the writer himself. They are "learned" men, like Poe, given to isolation while studying strange, remote subjects, rather than having "real-world" jobs. They fear for their sanity, as Poe apparently did.

The women in Poe's stories are cast from the same mold as well. While several of the tales are named for their ethereal women characters ("Ligeia," "Morella" and "Berenice," for example), the stories really center on the hero's love for these beautiful, accomplished women, extremely sensitive and not long for this world. Here again, the death of a beautiful woman is the melancholy theme, as the plot traces the hero's realization of and reaction to his tragic loss.

"The Fall of the House of Usher" is perhaps Poe's best Gothic story, as well as a perfect example of the way he uses every element, from the setting to the sounds of the words he chooses, to create a single effect:

> During the whole of a dull, dark, and soundless day in the autumn of the year, when the clouds hung oppressively low in the heavens, I had been passing alone, on horseback, through a singularly dreary tract of country, and at length found myself, as the shades of evening drew on, within view of the melancholy House of Usher.

The length of the sentence suggests the weariness of a long journey, and the reader is hardly surprised when, in the next sentence, the narrator confesses that when he saw the building, "a sense of insufferable gloom pervaded my spirit."

He goes on to detail his emotions:

> I looked upon the scene before me—upon the mere house, and the simple landscape features of the domain—upon the bleak walls—upon the vacant eye-like windows—upon a few rank sedges—and upon a few white trunks of decayed trees—with an utter depression of soul which I can compare to no earthly sensation more properly than to the after-dream of the reveller upon opium—the bitter lapse into every-day life—the hideous dropping off of the veil.

In addition to getting in many of the elements of Romanticism, this introduction to the story hints at the double meaning of the title. The phrase, "vacant eye-like windows" is a use of personification, in this case giving the house human qualities. The "House of Usher" is not only the physical home of a family named Usher. The term "House" is also the expression used for a dynasty, as an English monarch might be of "the House of York." The physical house is decaying and about to fall into the tarn (only Poe would call a lake a "tarn"), just as the last surviving members of the Usher family are also doomed to extinction.

In this story, Poe uses an unnamed first-person narrator to relate a story secondhand. The main characters, Roderick and Madeline Usher, cannot tell their own tragic story, since they do not survive the collapse of their house. But the narrator can, and does.

"MS Found in a Bottle" is another tale in which there were no survivors. Poe solved the narrative problem by having one of the participants write the details, then seal the paper into a bottle and throw it into the sea just as his vessel is overwhelmed by disaster.

Among other Poe stories, a few are surprisingly humorous. In "The Devil in the Belfry," "Never Bet the Devil Your Head," "The Duc de l'Omelette" and "Bon-Bon," Poe uses the devil as an ironic figure of fun. These grotesque stories never achieved the success of the other tales, however, and are rarely read today.

Edgar Allan Poe can certainly be classified as a Romantic writer. Yet, an element of logical thinking enters into even his most wildly emotional poetry and tales, so Poe took his natural talent for analysis one step further, and came up with an entirely new type of fiction.

With his usual love of large words, Poe labeled his new kind of fiction as tales of "ratiocination"—but today we call them detective stories.

THE LOGICAL ROMANTIC

In 1828, a series of stories titled "Unpublished Passages in the Life of Vidocq, the French Minister of Police" appeared in *Burton's Magazine*. Poe read these stories and was inspired to improve upon them. He created a fictional detective called C. Auguste Dupin, borrowing the last name from a character in one of the Vidocq stories. Dupin wasn't a professional policeman, but a scholarly amateur detective who solved crimes by using analysis, or "ratiocination." His methods included carefully examining the crime scene, then reviewing all the facts to arrive at a logical conclusion.

Poe's first ratiocinative tale, "The Murders in the Rue Morgue," appeared in *Graham's Magazine* in April 1841, the month in which Poe became its editor. Poe introduces the crime to the reader by a newspaper account, then proceeds with the witnesses at the inquest. One of them is an acquaintance of Dupin, who narrates the story in the first person. It is perhaps no coincidence that Dupin's mental powers bear a strong resemblance to Poe's own:

> As the strong man exults in his physical ability, delighting in such exercises as call his muscles into action, so glories the analyst in that moral activity which disentangles. He derives pleasure from even the most trivial occupations bringing his talent into play. He is fond of enigmas, of conundrums, hieroglyphics; exhibiting in his solutions of each a degree of acumen which appears to the ordinary apprehension preternatural.

In his tales of deduction, Poe takes the reader along as Dupin, the detective, looks for the unusual elements that will lead to a solution to the problem. The readers are told only what Poe wants them to know, making it impossible for them to arrive at the final outcome in advance.

In "The Murders in the Rue Morgue," a woman and her daughter have been brutally murdered under very mysterious circumstances, apparently without motivation. The police are puzzled by the crime. They know only that someone with great strength committed it. Witnesses reported hearing a Frenchman shouting to someone who spoke in a shrill, harsh voice in a language the witnesses did not understand.

After examining the evidence and visiting the crime scene, Dupin concludes that the murder was committed by an "ourang-outang," or orangutan. A sailor confesses that he had brought the animal to Paris to sell, but it escaped. He had followed the large ape and seen the murder through the apartment window, but was unable to do anything to prevent it. As a result of this confession, an innocent man who had been accused of the crime is set free, and the recaptured orangutan is sold to a zoo.

In "The Philosophy of Composition," Poe relates the method he uses in all his tales, but particularly those which involve logic. Charles Dickens had written Poe, "By the way, are you aware that Godwin wrote his *Caleb Williams* backward? He first involved his hero in a web of difficulties, forming the second volume, and then, for the first, cast about him for some mode of accounting for what had been done." Poe says that the Dickens comment points out the necessity for an author to write the ending of a story first, then work backward, carefully selecting the details which will lead to that final result.

Like most writers, Edgar Allan Poe's ideas came from many sources. He observed and remembered even the smallest of details, and he read extensively. In 1837 and 1838, when Poe lived in New York, he often visited a tobacco shop whose patrons included successful writers like James Fenimore Cooper. There he met a beautiful salesgirl named Mary Cecilia Rogers. Three years later, the girl's battered and strangled body was found in the Hudson River. Newspapers were filled with stories about the case for months. Poe saved the clippings and, in 1842, he began a sequel to "The Murders in the Rue Morgue" in which he attempted to solve in fiction the mystery of a murder that still puzzled the New York City police.

Poe personally knew the suspects in the case, and he was aware that the girl had mysteriously disappeared for a time in October 1838. He decided the murderer must have been a naval officer aboard a man o' war, since the time between Mary's first disappearance and the murder was three years— the length of an ordinary cruise on such a vessel.

Poe cast the known facts into the mold of fiction in "The Mystery of Marie Roget." A beautiful Parisienne leaves her home, telling her mother she is going to see an aunt. Four days later, her body is found in the Seine. The Prefect of Police offers amateur detective C. Auguste Dupin a reward if he can solve the case.

One suspect is proved innocent only after he commits suicide, and, by use of logic, Dupin shows that another suspect could not have been the murderer. Dupin deduces that a secret lover committed the crime. He threw Marie's body from a boat and, after reaching shore, cast the boat adrift. When police found the boat and examined it for clues, the mystery was solved.

In real life, the chief suspect in Mary Rogers' death committed suicide in 1841. A sailor who could have been the one Poe suspected (and whose name he never revealed) was later hanged from the yardarm of his vessel for conspiracy to mutiny.

The third and final of the Dupin ratiocinative tales, "The Purloined Letter," is generally considered Poe's best. No murder is involved, but once more the baffled Prefect of Police must call on Dupin for help. A potentially damaging letter is missing, and the Prefect has failed in his attempts to find it.

The Prefect fails, Poe suggests, because he lacks the imagination to think like a culprit, which Dupin can—and does. Rather than being hidden in some clever way, as the police assume, the missing letter—somewhat stained and crumpled as if of no consequence—has been left out in plain sight with other mail. It is so obvious, in fact, that in effect it is hidden.

Realizing this, Dupin prepares a dummy letter, identical to the one that must be recovered, and then returns to the culprit's apartment. An accomplice creates a disturbance that causes the man to look outside to see what is happening. His back is turned on Dupin just long enough for the detective to replace the real letter with the one made to look like it. The purloined (stolen) letter is safely retrieved, thanks to the cleverness of Dupin.

Poe's detective stories use several devices that are now so familiar that they are taken for granted. But it was Poe who originated them. One of these could be called "the device of the baffled friend." The stories are told in the first person, not by Dupin, but by an unnamed narrator who lacks the brilliant detective's ratiocinative abilities. In the British writer Sir Arthur Conan Doyle's stories, Sherlock Holmes is the observant detective who patiently explains his conclusions to his companion, Dr. Watson.

Another of Poe's devices comes at the end of the tales, when Dupin announces his surprising solution and then explains the reasoning leading to it. The Sherlock Holmes stories employ this method, as have literally hundreds of later fictional detectives who gather all the suspects into one room before revealing the real murderer.

Poe might have never offered his analytical talents to the police, but he applied them to many kinds of problems. When he was editor of *Graham's Magazine* he wrote a series of articles about cryptography (writing messages in code). He claimed to have challenged readers of *Alexander's Weekly Messenger* to send him a cryptogram that he would be unable to decipher. Poe said he had received about a hundred messages in code, and solved all but one of them, which he proved was impossible to solve.

Poe's interest in such puzzles is clear in "The Gold-Bug," a tale in which buried pirate treasure is found through deciphering a cryptogram. Poe leads readers step by step through the thought processes of an unnamed first-person narrator as he uncovers the meaning of the cryptogram. The cipher is a simple one in which a letter is always represented by the same character. The reader is told that "e" is the most frequently used letter in the English alphabet, followed in order by a, o, i, d, h, n, r, s, t, u, y, c, f, g, l, m, w, b, k, p, q, x, and z. Therefore, the symbol most often used in the cryptogram must refer to "e," and since "the" is the most-used word in the language, he logically then looks for repeating patterns that represent those three letters. The complete explanation of the cryptogram goes on for several pages, until the message on the pirate's map clearly leads to the exact spot where the treasure is found.

During his time as editor of *The Southern Literary Messenger*, Edgar Allan Poe wrote about a mechanical device called "Maelzel's Chess-Player" which was made to look like a Turk. It had created quite a sensation when first exhibited in Philadelphia in 1827, and had toured a number of American cities. Several articles had been written in an attempt to solve the problem presented by an automaton that seemed capable of thought.

Poe applied logic to the material that had already been printed and proved by reasoning that the "device" was nothing more than a machine with a man hidden inside it. He selected the unusual elements in the problem, among them that the Turk always used his left hand.

In addition to taking things apart to solve a problem, Poe could also reverse the process and build up something from nothing and make it seem true. Such was "The Balloon-Hoax," which appeared in the *New York Sun* in 1844.

The story began with a headline, as if it were a factual newspaper account:

"ASTOUNDING NEWS BY EXPRESS, VIA NORFOLK! THE ATLANTIC CROSSED IN THREE DAYS! SIGNAL TRIUMPH OF MR. MONCK MASON'S FLYING MACHINE!"

Using academic jargon, Poe describes the balloon that made this crossing and quotes from the journal kept by "aeronaut" Harrison Ainsworth. He goes into great detail about the craft's complicated navigation. Only when neither reporters nor anyone else could find Ainsworth or the balloon he supposedly piloted did it become obvious that they never existed.

Poe's writing often went unappreciated in the United States, but he found a better audience in France. Around 1846 the poet and critic Charles Baudelaire discovered some of Poe's work and set out to translate all of Poe's tales into French. Baudelaire, who shared Poe's passion for art in literature, said, "I wish Poe, who is a nobody in America, to become a great man in France."

As a result of Baudelaire's efforts, Poe had a great influence on French poets like Stéphane Mallarmé and Paul Valéry. Poe's accounts of balloon and submarine voyages led Jules Verne to write similar stories. These tales represent the earliest form of what has come to be known as science fiction.

Baudelaire was all too correct in his assessment of Edgar Allan Poe as a literary "nobody" in America. The poverty that had pursued him all his adult life continued, made even worse by his wife's illness. The man now acclaimed as one of America's best and most original writers could not provide his adored Virginia with even the smallest comforts as her illness progressed.

Yet, when Poe moved his family to Fordham in 1846, he still nourished some hope that better days lay ahead.

THE CURTAIN BEGINS TO FALL

Edgar Allan Poe believed that going to live to Fordham, 13 miles from downtown New York City, would be a fresh start and that the country air would benefit Virginia's poor health. Fordham was then an area with farmhouses and cottages along the Kingsbridge Highway. Lilac bushes and a cherry tree stood between the house and road. The house had only three rooms on the first floor and two more in an unheated attic, but it offered a view of St. John's College to the southeast, and from a nearby hill, the Long Island hills beyond the East River. Later, Poe described the house in his story, "Landor's Cottage." A woman named Mrs. Gove visited Poe in 1846, accompanied by George Colton, the editor who had taken "The Raven." She wrote:

> We found him, and his wife, and his wife's mother—who was his aunt—living in a little cottage at the top of a hill . . . There was a piazza in front of the house that was a lovely place to sit in the summer. . . . There was no cultivation, no flowers—nothing but the smooth greensward and the majestic trees. . . . On this occasion, I was introduced to the young wife of the poet, and to the mother, then more than 60 years of age. She was a tall, dignified lady . . . and it seemed strange how such a stalwart and queenly woman could be the mother of her almost petite daughter. Mrs. Poe looked very young; she had large black eyes, and a pearly whiteness of complexion, which was a perfect pallor. Her pale face, her brilliant eyes, and her raven hair gave her an unearthly look. One felt she was almost a disrobed spirit, and

when she coughed it was made certain that she was rapidly passing away. . . . The cottage had an air of taste and gentility. . . . So neat, so poor, so unfurnished, and yet so charming a dwelling I never saw.

During that visit, Mrs. Clemm begged George Colton to buy a poem that "Eddie" had written. It was "Ulalume," a "loss" poem set in a typical Poe dreamland that was far different from the area in which he actually lived. "Ulalume" opens with these lines:

> The skies they were ashen and sober:
> The leaves they were crispéd and sere—
> The leaves they were withering and sere;
> It was night in the lonesome October
> Of my most immemorial year.
>
> It was hard by the dim lake of Auber,
> In the misty mid region of Weir—
> It was down by the dank tarn of Auber,
> In the ghoul-haunted woodland of Weir ...

George Colton paid Poe for the poem that day, although it wasn't published until December 1847.

In the winter of 1846 Poe's worst fears concerning the ultimate result of Virginia's illness were about to be realized. The move to Fordham hadn't helped, and Poe's poverty only made his wife's suffering more acute. Mrs. Gove gives this report of a further visit to the cottage at Fordham:

> The autumn came, and Mrs. Poe sank rapidly in consumption, and I saw her in her bedchamber. Everything here was so neat, so purely clean, so scant and poverty-stricken. . . . There was no clothing on the bed, which was only straw, but a snow white spread and sheets. The weather was cold, and the sick lady had the dreadful chills that accompany the hectic fever of consumption. She lay on the bed, wrapped in her husband's great-coat, with a large tortoise-shell cat on her bosom. . . . The coat and the cat were the sufferer's only means of warmth, except as her husband held her hands, and her mother her feet.

Mrs. Gove told others of the Poe family's plight, and several people came to their assistance. Poe keenly resented having to take charity, but for his wife's sake, he did so.

On January 30, 1847, Virginia lost her long fight for life. She was buried on February 2, and Poe collapsed under the strain. Mrs. Marie Louise Shew, who had helped nurse Virginia, turned her attention to him. She consulted a prominent physician about his symptoms, and later wrote:

> I decided that in his best health he [Poe] had lesion of one side of the brain . . . he could not bear stimulants or tonics, without producing insanity. . . . I did not feel much hope that he could be raised up from brain fever brought on by extreme suffering of mind and body—actual want and hunger, and cold having been borne by this heroic husband in order to supply food, medicine, and comforts to his dying wife . . .

Whether the cause of his illness was "brain fever" or simply the effects grief took on his spirit, Poe was devastated.

He threw himself into work on *Eureka*, a long-prose poem dealing with the meaning of the universe, and he still hoped to have a magazine of his own. *Eureka* was published in the summer of 1848 by George Putnam. Not all of the 500 copies that were printed were actually sold. *Eureka* was ahead of its time, as Poe discussed matters more in the realm of theoretical physics than literature. The work puzzled the few who read it, and it did not provide him with the hoped-for income.

Poe continued to live in the Fordham cottage with his aunt, Maria Clemm, who shared in his grief over Virginia's death and to whom he had always felt close. He had lost both his birth mother and Frances Allan by the time he came to know his aunt, and Poe grew to regard her as the mother he had never had. In tribute to Maria Clemm, Poe wrote "A Sonnet—To My Mother," which ends with these lines:

> My mother—my own mother, who died early,
> Was but the mother of myself; but you
> Are mother to the one I loved so dearly,
> And thus are dearer than the mother I knew
> By that infinity with which my wife
> Was dearer to my soul than its soul-life.

In the months following Virginia's death, Poe became romantically involved with several women who offered him sympathy and comfort. One of these women was Mrs. Sarah Helen Power Whitman, described as an attractive widow, for whom he wrote a second poem with the title "To Helen." A fellow writer of poetry, Mrs. Whitman lived in Providence, Rhode

Island. Poe first saw her in 1845, but they did not meet until 1848. After an exchange of letters, they became engaged to be married. However, her family raised objections, which added to Mrs. Whitman's own doubts, and the planned wedding never took place.

Another woman who attracted Poe's attention and inspired a poem ("To Annie") was Nancy Locke Heywood Richmond, a married woman who lived in Lowell, Massachusetts. Poe met her while lecturing there in June 1848 and fell in love with her. Poe urged her to move to New York so she would be closer to him, but she apparently never had any intention of leaving her husband. In addition to his poem to her, Poe made "Annie" a character in his story, "Landor's Cottage." In it he described his first impression of her as a slender young woman about 28 years of age from whose deep-set eyes gleamed a fascinating "unworldliness."

All this time, Poe continued to write. "The Bells," published in 1849, would become one of his most famous poems. Its masterful use of onomatopoeia (the use of a word whose sound suggests its meaning) indicates that the poet was still able to achieve "the rhythmical creation of beauty."

In the spring of 1849, Edgar Allan Poe composed what was to be his last poem, "Annabel Lee," published only after Poe's death. The poet's favorite theme of lost love is at its most poignant as Poe writes, in part:

> . . . we loved with a love that was more than love—
>   I and my Annabel Lee—
> With a love that the wingéd seraphs of Heaven
>   Coveted her and me.
> And this was the reason that, long ago,
>   In this kingdom by the sea,
> A wind blew out of a cloud chilling
>   beautiful Annabel Lee . . .
> The angels, not half so happy in Heaven
>   Went envying her and me:
> Yes! that was the reason (as all men know,
>   In this kingdom by the sea)
> That the wind came out of a cloud by night,
> Chilling and killing my Annabel Lee,
> But our love it was stronger by far then the love
>   Of those who were older than we—
> And neither the angels in Heaven above
>   Nor the demons down under the sea,
> Can ever dissever my soul from the soul
>   Of the beautiful Annabel Lee: . . .

Poe's last poem addresses the same theme as had "Tamerlane," his first poem—youthful love that lasts beyond death. No matter what the circumstances, Edgar Allan Poe never lost his Romantic belief in the enduring power of love.

In the summer of 1849, Edgar Allan Poe began a southern tour lecturing on "The Poetic Principle." It was a means of earning funds to start a magazine, which he intended to call the *Stylus*. He went to Richmond, where his sister Rosalie still lived with the Mackenzies, the family who had taken her in so many years ago.

There Poe also renewed his acquaintance with Sarah Elmira Royster Shelton, now a widow. Resuming their youthful romance, Poe asked Sarah Elmira to marry him. Although by the terms of her late husband's will she would give up a large part of her inheritance if she remarried, by late August Sarah Elmira had accepted Poe's proposal.

Poe's alcoholism had been an issue with many of his employers and had been part of the reason Sarah Elmira left him when they were young. Now, in an attempt to appease her, he joined the Sons of Temperance, a society that required its members to abstain completely from drinking alcoholic beverages.

The date for Poe's marriage to Mrs. Shelton was set for October 17, 1849. Poe planned to return to New York, by boat, to bring Mrs. Clemm to Richmond for the wedding. It is known that Edgar Allan Poe boarded the boat for Baltimore at four o'clock on the morning of September 27, apparently in good condition. But what happened to him from that time until October 3 is shrouded in mystery and conjecture.

Apparently Poe arrived in Baltimore on the morning of September 28 and tried to call on someone who was not at home. One account says that he went on to Philadelphia, where he became ill and spent the night with a friend. Against that friend's protests, Poe left Philadelphia in rather poor condition, probably on September 30. He should have gone by train to New York, but somehow wound up in Baltimore.

On October 3, a Baltimore printer named Walker sent this letter to Poe's friend Dr. J. E. Snodgrass, also in Baltimore:

Dear Sir:
     There is a gentleman rather worse for wear, at Ryan's 4th Ward Polls, who goes under the cognomen of Edgar A. Poe, and who appears in great distress, and he says he is acquainted with you, and I assure you he is in need of immediate assistance.

Dr. Snodgrass found Poe at a public house, and he and Henry Herring, the husband of Poe's aunt, Elizabeth Poe, took him to Washington College

Hospital on the afternoon of October 3. In a semiconscious condition, Poe was delirious and unable to tell anyone what had happened to him. On October 4, Poe's Baltimore cousin Neilson Poe, who had once offered to care for Maria and Virginia Clemm, called on Poe at the hospital, but was not allowed to see him.

Edgar Allan Poe died at five o'clock on Sunday morning, October 7, 1849. His burial took place at 4:30 the next afternoon, in a lot that had belonged to his grandfather, David Poe, in the Presbyterian cemetery. Neilson Poe paid for the hack and hearse, and the Reverend William D. Clemm, another Poe relative, conducted the funeral. The weather was cold and gray, with a touch of rain, as the mahogany coffin provided by Poe's uncle, Henry Herring, a lumber dealer, was lowered into the ground. Present were Henry Herring, Neilson Poe, Dr. J. E. Snodgrass, and Z. Collins Lee, a University of Virginia classmate and lifelong friend of Poe.

The cause of Poe's death has been the subject of much discussion and controversy over the years. Some think that Poe had been drinking heavily and passed out in a waterfront saloon, dying of acute alcohol poisoning. The fact that Poe was wearing clothes which were not his own led his own doctor to believe that he might have been robbed and beaten up by thugs. Another theory claims that, since elections were going on in Baltimore at the time, someone could have drugged Poe or given him some drinks and dressed him a different suit of clothes so he could cast an illegal vote.

Medical doctors have speculated that the description of Poe at his death could be accounted for by a weak heart aggravated by drinking, or that he might have been in a diabetic coma. He also had symptoms of encephalitis. One of the most recent theories holds that details of his final illness point to the possibility that Poe might have been bitten by a rabid dog or cat (he was especially fond of cats) and actually died from rabies.

After his death, Poe's reputation was greatly damaged by Rufus Griswold, the man he had chosen as his literary executor. Apparently jealous of Poe's ability, Griswold tampered with Poe's letters in order to malign him, while Griswold painted himself as Poe's benefactor. Over the years, many of the Griswold's untruths or damaging half-truths have made their way into Poe biographies and have contributed to the folklore that has sprung up about him as a drug-crazed fiend.

The Edgar Allan Poe Society of Baltimore has classified three distinct "camps," or schools of thought, seen in Edgar Allan Poe's critics, each named for its originator. Rufus Griswold presented Poe as an alcoholic with an immoral nature. Therefore, the "Griswold Camp" vilifies Poe as a devil.

John H. Ingram wrote critical studies and a biography that is highly complimentary, so the "Ingram Camp" tends to glorify Poe as an angel.

Finally, the French writer Charles Baudelaire admired a dark side of Poe that reflected his own feelings. Thus, the "Baudelaire Camp" glorifies Poe as a devil.

No matter what his biographers say about him, Poe's life and works have remained a constant source of fascination to readers all over the world. It is not surprising, then, that so many of the sites where Edgar Allan Poe lived and worked have been preserved and are now open to the public.

COURTNEY J. RUFFNER AND JEFF GRIENEISEN

Intelligence: Genius or Insanity? Tracing Motifs in Poe's Madness Tales

While critical treatments of Edgar Allan Poe have included such topics as Charles E. May's rhetorical approach of reader response criticism, and J.M. Cohen's and John Curtis's psychological approach, a perspective that is often overlooked is how Poe confuses the reader's sense of whether his narrator is mad or trustworthy. In questioning the definition of madness, Poe, himself, pondered "whether madness [was] or [was] not the loftiest intelligence—whether all that [was] profound—[did] not spring from disease of thought. . ." (May 66). Because the narrator in so many of Poe's tales presents himself as a perfectly stable source by explaining, in great detail, how his intellect has helped him to make wise decisions throughout his life, we find ourselves questioning the narrator's credibility.

Although researchers have given us a foundation on which to build, the definition of madness is not yet settled. Poe said that the *disease* from which his characters suffer in these madness stories is that of monomania "consisting of a 'morbid irritability of those properties of the mind in metaphysical science termed the *attentive*'"(May 65). Following this line of reasoning, the reader can see that Poe considered madness a purely intellectual entanglement. In *From the Marginalia*, Poe wrote an essay titled, "Great Wit To Madness Is Nearly Allied . . ." where he asserts his views on the criteria for a talented writer:

"genius"—that "genius" in the popular sense—which is but the manifestation of the abnormal predominance of some one faculty over all the others—and of course at the detriment, of all the others—is a result of mental disease or rather, of organic malformation of mind: it is this and nothing more . . . The proportion of the mental faculties, in a case where the general mental power is *not* inordinate, gives that result which we distinguish as *talent*. (Foye 37, 38)

Thus, Poe admits in his own personal essays that the very "disease" of the mind that we call to question when reading his tales stems simply from "genius." This unusual portrayal of genius provides the foundation for the insanity discussion. If genius is a result of madness, and to be considered a talented writer one must be a genius, then, according to Poe, all talented writers are mad.

While we consider that Poe wrote this as his personal philosophy, we must also take into consideration David Halliburton's discussion on Poe's enjoyment at "hoaxing the public." Indeed, we may have uncovered a portion of Poe's philosophy concerning his criteria for evaluating a talented writer, but we must not fail to view Poe's paradoxical epistemology. In Poe's fiction as well as in his personal essays, he contradicts his own phrases (in some instances he contradicts himself in the very next sentence). In the same essay on madness, Poe continues with his views on "genius":

Not only will such 'genius' fail, if turned aside from the path indicated by its predominant faculty; but, even when pursuing this path—when producing those works in which, certainly, it is best calculated to succeed—will give unmistakable indications of *unsoundness*, in respect to general intellect. (Foye 37)

By reading this portion of the madness essay against the first portion, we can be sure of two properties: Poe not only understood the concept of madness, but he had his own epistemology concerning the criteria for its evaluation. Moreover, Poe used this criteria to self-evaluate his own writing.

While Poe's writing is considered representative of American Romanticism, characterized by heightened sensations, embellished feelings, and a confused sense of reality, we must acknowledge the idea that Poe is a writer with many facets. He can be considered a serious writer or an "active inventor of mysteries" (Halliburton 229). When analyzing Poe, we need to be able to determine whether he wrote his tales to be taken seriously or whether he decided to play a hoax on his readers by including in his tales outrageous plots, unbelievable endings, and contradictory narrators.

Oftentimes, the narrators in Poe's tales are presented in a paradoxical way. One of these paradoxes is that of the insane/sane narrator. In "The Black Cat," the narrator appears insane because of his unjustified reactions to his life; yet the tale never admits to the narrator's sanity. The narrator in "The Tell-Tale Heart" actually tells us that he is insane, but then "the [tale] invites us to find a method to the narrator's madness" (Peeples 94). The narrator tells us the entire story of how he kills the old man "calmly" and "healthily" (both the telling of the story and the murder), but yet we are expected to believe he is insane. What we need are a few working definitions of insanity in order to distinguish between the sane and the insane in Poe's tales.

Physician J. C. Prichard introduces the term "moral insanity" as a special type of illness. He calls it:

> . . . madness consisting in a morbid perversion of the natural feelings, affections, inclinations, temper, habits, and moral dispositions and natural impulses without any remarkable disorder or defect in the intellect or knowing and reasoning faculties and particularly without any insane illusion or hallucination. (qtd. in Meinsma n. pag.)

From this definition the reader interprets the narrator in Poe's madness stories as "insane." Prichard's criteria of moral insanity, representative of 19th century views, unveils distinctions between ideas of irrationality, unreason, eccentric or irrational behavior, and the significance of anxiety/guilt in the determination of madness.

In the 18th century, one connotation of the word "mad" was that the character was angry. In Poe's own era, the definition seemed clear; if a narrator wrote that a character was "mad," then that character possessed certain qualities of insanity. According to acclaimed early 20th century psychiatrist George Rosen, M.D., in the 19th century:

> reason provided the norm; any divergence from the norm was irrational . . . Descartes recognized that reason and irrationality are encountered together and dreams and errors are associated with madness. . . . (Rosen 164–65)

From this we can determine that irrationality and unreason/insanity were believed to be a matter of choice and volition, and were not the integrity of the rational mind. Rosen also points out that "eccentric or irrational behavior was considered as rooted in error or as derangements of the will."

In conjunction with Prichard's ideas of insanity, Rosen further asserts that anxiety/guilt is also a significant element contributing to insanity. For example, the anxiety that one feels when over stressed from lack of sleep causes the mind to peak *hallucinogenically* into a dream–like trance (Rosen 61–2). According to Rosen, this hallucinogenic behavior was considered, in Poe's time, a psychological disorder probed by "an oppressive sense of guilt and an unconscious desire for self-punishment."

Poe demonstrates both the irrational and the anxious elements in his section of short stories dealing with madness. "The Black Cat," "The Tell-Tale Heart," and "Eleonora" are good examples of his manipulation of his reader's conscious and unconscious mind. "Eleonora" may be the most effective example of this control, because although Poe's narrator manipulates the reader into trusting him, the pattern of insanity prevails throughout this tale. Poe uses rhetorical disclaimers to confuse this idea of insanity, and, in turn, manages to trick his readers into trusting the narrators. Although Prichard's definition suggests that there are no insane illusions or hallucinations to be detected in the stability of the accused, Poe's narrator fits all of Prichard's remaining criteria. This definition provides the context necessary to analyze the sanity/insanity claim in Poe's tales, and to illustrate that Poe used the narrators shifting sanity to manipulate his readers into questioning the very nature of sanity and reliability.

I.

From the very first lines of "The Black Cat," the narrator simultaneously creates doubt about his sanity and tries to win the reader's sympathy and convince the reader of his sanity:

> For the most wild yet most homely narrative which I am about to pen, I neither expect nor solicit belief. Mad indeed would I be to expect it, in a case where my very senses reject their own evidence. Yet, mad am I not—and very surely do I not dream. But tomorrow I die, and to-day I would unburden my soul.

Here the narrator tells his readers that while the narrative may seem wild, it is also his true narrative. The narrator describes the story as wild yet homely to illustrate that he is, indeed, sane, or "wild," but grounded. The narrator insists that he is neither mad nor dreaming, which is also supposed to illustrate his sanity. While he does not expect his readers to believe his story, he must tell it. However, the narrator's need to "unburden his soul" causes the reader to question his sanity early in the narrative, because such a confession implies guilt, one cause of a person's detachment from his/her mind. On the conscious level, the narrator himself seems to be aware that he is substituting his reader for a priest in a confessional in order to "unburden" his soul before his death. Rhetorically, this confessional tone seems to be calculated to induce belief in the narrator's sincerity.

In the second paragraph, the narrator pleads for sympathy by indicating, "From my infancy I was noted for the docility and humanity of my disposition." Because of his gentle childhood manner and particularly because of his fondness for animals, he appears incapable of harming any living thing. This fondness and compassion for animals prompts the narrator and his wife to own many pets, including a cat that was:

> remarkably large and beautiful animal, entirely black, and sagacious to an astonishing degree. In speaking of his intelligence, my wife, who at heart was not a little tinctured with superstition, made frequent allusion to the ancient popular notion, which regarded all black cats as witches in disguise. Not that she was ever *serious* upon this point—and I mention the matter at all for no better reason than that it happens, just now, to be remembered.

Here again the narrator tries to validate his own sanity, this time by placing himself in the position of the sane and rational husband who had means to comment on his wife's superstition. He raises the issue of the supernatural (superstition) in the mind of the reader only to eliminate it by casual dismissal. By this dismissal, the narrator validates his sanity.

This sanity is further validated two paragraphs later when the narrator calmly relates his mood alterations. He even acts embarrassed; he "blush[es] to confess it." Yet in this paragraph the narrator begins to lose his composure. The repetition of words "even Pluto" and the relegation of Pluto as victim of the narrator's ire indicates the narrator's descent into madness. Here the narrator hallucinates Pluto, who, "becoming old, and consequently somewhat peevish—[. . .] began to experience the effects of [his] ill-temper."

The narrator's inarguable descent into insanity is marked by his "damnable atrocity" of gouging out the cat's eyes. Drunk and in a rage, the narrator relates, "I knew myself no longer. My original soul seemed at once to take its flight from my body." If he did not know himself and in fact, his soul had left his body, then his "madness," if it can yet be deemed so, is not his. Instead, "[t]he fury of a demon instantly possessed [him]." By shifting the responsibility of this action (and perhaps then of all of his actions), the narrator counteracts our impulse to regard him as insane.

While his pleas of sanity evaporate, the narrator claims that he is sane and that his mental disposition is vexed only because of the effects of alcohol. After all, he is drunk when he commits his horrible "atrocity." The demon causes him to commit the act, and alcohol (or its effects) troubles his mood.

Another way that the narrator convinces the reader of his sanity is by displaying rational intelligence. He puzzles the nature of perversity, insisting:

> I am more sure that my soul lives, than I am that perverseness is one of the primitive impulses of the human heart— one of the indivisible primary faculties, or sentiment, which give direction to the character of man. Who has not, a hundred times, found himself committing a vile or a stupid action, for no other reason than because he knows he should not?

Philosophical and intelligent, the beginning of the passage indicates that the narrator is digging for peace of mind, perhaps even using these lines as a ploy to gain sympathy. By the end of the passage, he justifies his act. This logical appeal to the reader's commission of such acts endears the reader to the narrator and negates the narrator's guilt. After all, every man has committed "vile" acts because he knows he should not do them.

The narrator's descent into madness hastens one night as he sits drinking in his den. He notices on a hogshead of gin in his apartment:

> It was a black cat—a very large one—fully as large as Pluto, and closely resembling him in every respect but one. Pluto had not a white hair upon any portion of his body; but this cat had a large, although indefinite splotch of white, covering nearly the whole region of the beast.

The narrator's fondness for the new/hallucinated pet turned to annoyance and eventually into hatred. Here, the hallucination of the cat and Pluto combine to create a sense of detachment from reality.

Eventually, the narrator becomes overcome by evil thoughts. In fact, something *evil* has taken over, and "[t]he moodiness of [his] usual temper increased to hatred of all things and of all mankind." His temper has risen to an uncontrollable level, and even his wife, who still has not complained about his disposition, becomes a victim of his violent side. The narrator's recognition of his wife as "the most patient of sufferers" indicates that he has already passed the threshold of insanity. The narrator prides himself on retaining his composure throughout the narrative. In fact, it is this composure that causes the narrator to believe his own sanity. Yet his consciousness of the patient suffering his wife endures, his calm recollection of this suffering woman he loves, shows his detachment and the lack of sympathy on which he recently prided himself. The contradiction, then, lies in the narrator's words and actions, for while he calmly tells the tale, the tale he tells is one of himself in a rage and is not as plausible as he would like us to believe.

The narrator again justifies his perverse actions by focusing on the evil of the cat. He relates that while going to the cellar, "[t]he cat followed [. . . and] exasperated [him] to madness." The narrator's uncontrollable rage was further instigated by his wife who "goaded" the narrator "into a rage more than demoniacal[.] [He] withdrew [his] arm from her grasp and buried the axe in her brain." Therefore, because of the demon cat and the interference of his wife that "exasperated [him] to madness," he is in his own mind exonerated of the murder. The narrator's calculated logic reaches its climax when he relates his considerations in disposing of the body. Here, the narrator explains the great details and logical conclusions he considered. At this point, the narrator is clearly mad according to Prichard's definition of moral insanity. The narrator explains:

> Many projects entered my mind. At one period I thought of cutting the corpse into minute fragments, and destroying them by fire. At another, I resolved to dig a grave for it in the floor of the cellar. Again, I deliberated about casting it in the well in the yard—about packing it in a box, as if merchandise, with the usual arrangements, and so getting a porter to take it from the house. Finally I hit upon what I considered a far better expedient than either of these. I determined to wall it up in the cellar, as the monks of the Middle Ages are recorded to have walled up their victims.

These thoughts demonstrate a kind of sane logic that causes the reader to think that perhaps since the narrator is so logical, then the narrator is also sane. Such precise intellect confuses the reader's perception of sanity. However, we can define the narrator as morally insane by Prichard's insistence that the "feelings," "temper," and "moral dispositions" may be perverse, while his intellect remains sharp as ever. The insane enjoy faculties of reason; instead, the manner of telling indicates the insanity. The fact that the narrator can calmly relate how he entombed the corpse eliminates doubt that he has gone mad. A sane person would become remorseful.

Eventually, however, the narrator must feel something of his own crime, his own madness. After the murder, the narrator feels relief from both the absence of the cat and the police investigation that turns up nothing. The narrator slept even with "the burden of murder on [his] soul." However, the narrator continues to lose credibility, if he indeed retains any by this point, when he confesses to us, "The glee at my heart was too strong to be restrained. I burned to say if but one word, by way of triumph, and to render doubly sure their assurance of my guiltlessness." Here his madness has penetrated his morality.

Eventually, the narrator's ramblings betray his sanity. The moral insanity that once held him together, that once enabled him to appear rational, now causes his psychological unraveling as he attempts to validate his innocence. The repetition of *this—this* and *These walls— these walls* on the last page becomes the visual evidence in the case of the narrator's downfall. This repetition shows the narrator's shaken disposition. This struggle between guilt driven by the murder and insanity knocking the last shred of guiltless peace out of the narrator's mind peaks in the narrator's prayer:

> 'But may God shield and deliver me from the fangs of the Arch—
> Fiend! . . . one long, loud, and continuous scream, utterly
> anomalous and inhuman—a howl—a wailing shriek, half of
> horror and half of triumph, such as might have arisen only out of
> hell.'

The narrator repents aloud and is answered by "a voice within the tomb." The voice is literally the sound of the cat meowing. Symbolically, the voice is the narrator's conscience. Phrases like: "possession of [my] body by a familiar force, the Arch—Fiend," "the damned in their agony," and "the demons that exult in the damnation" all serve as representations of how the narrator's mind is consumed with guilt. This guilt increases to the point of paranoid hallucinations, as the narrator believes that the cat's screaming horrified the police party. The narrator continues to denounce the cat as the cause of the murder even after the police have discovered the truth. The narrator describes the cat as the ". . . beast whose craft had seduced me into murder. . . ."

A reader may question at what point the narrator goes mad, but there remains no doubt that he does, indeed, go mad. From the beginning of the tale the narrator reinforces his sanity by claiming, "I neither select nor solicit belief . . . mad I am not—and very sure I do not dream. . . ." His pleas for sympathy, the dismissal of superstition, and the composure demonstrated when concealing the body and explaining why the cellar was the perfect place to conceal it all further confuse the issue as to whether the narrator is insane or sane.

II.

Although the narrator of "The Tell-Tale Heart" is fully aware of the heinousness of his act, he commits the murderous deed anyway. Like the narrator in *The Black Cat*, this narrator begins by trying to convince the reader of his sanity and authority:

> TRUE!—nervous—very, very dreadfully nervous I had been and am; but why *will* you say that I am mad? The disease had sharpened my senses—not destroyed—not dulled them. Above all was the sense of hearing acute. I heard all things in the heaven and in the earth. I heard many things in hell. How, then, am I mad? Hearken! and observe how healthily—how calmly I can tell you the whole story.

Here, however, the narrator admits to having a "disease," which the reader may interpret as insanity. The narrator's questioning ". . . why *will* you say that I am mad? . . . How, then, am I mad?" and his demand for attention: "observe how healthily—how calmly I can tell you the whole story," indicate his anxiety—the same anxiety that, at the end of the tale, betrays his innocence to the police. The italicized "*will*" in his question emphasizes the narrator's awareness that the reader already presumes him to be mad. Had the narrator emphasized "why," he would have indicated that he was surprised by someone accusing him of madness. Instead, he knows he is called mad, and his reason for telling the tale is to plead his sanity.

The victims of both tales are characters beloved to the narrators. The narrator of "The Tell-Tale Heart" says that the man never did him wrong, and the narrator did not desire any of his money. Just as in "The Black Cat," the narrator needs to find an object of evil onto which he can project his own idea of insanity. This way the narrator appeals to the reader's sense that something can drive a normally sane person to an otherwise unheard-of action. In "The Black Cat" this object was the cat; in "The Tell-Tale Heart" this object is the old man's eye. Here the narrator relates:

> I think it was his eye! yes, it was this! One of his eyes resembled that of a vulture—a pale blue eye, with a film over it. Whenever it fell upon me, my blood ran cold; and so by degrees—very gradually—I made up my mind to take the life of the old man, and thus rid myself of the eye forever.

Again, the issue of moral insanity—disorder of natural impulses without disorder in the intellect—emerges as the narrator calmly relates how he was driven to his deed.

While the narrator admits to knowing that he is seen as mad, he defends himself by stating, "madmen know nothing. But you should have seen *me*." He tells the story with such coherence that the readers could not possibly believe him to be crazy. Obsessive repetitions in this narrative, as in "The Black Cat," help to establish insane behavior patterns. The repetition of "closed," "very slowly," and "cautiously" throughout the description of the old man's bedroom supports the claim of the narrator's insanity by the obsessed disturbance of his mood. Although the narrator perceives himself as calm, he is, in fact, losing his composure. This lost composure speaks of the deterioration of the narrator's behavior, yet at no time does the narrator's logic deteriorate.

In addition to repetition indicating the narrator's insanity, the narrator's constant questioning causes the reader to question this sanity. The narrator boasts "Ha! —Would a madman have been so wise as this?" In this boast is not only the narrator's questioning of his own madness, but also the misconception that a mad man would not be wise. Because the reader knows that the morally insane may have a perfectly normal intellect, the use of such evidence to propose sanity is vacuous, and such vacuity calls into question the very authority and reliability of the narrator.

Like other descriptions, the narrator's particularly astute account of the events of the murder reveals his neurotic attention to detail. He indicates that his heightened level of awareness and increased consciousness of the act makes him sane. Again, the reader knows differently. The following account indicates the degree of the narrator's obsession with time and detail:

> Upon the eighth night I was more than usually cautious in opening the door. A watch's minute hand moves more quickly than did mine. . . . I had my head in, and was about to open the lantern, when my thumb slipped upon the tin fastening, and the old man sprang up in the bed, crying out—"Who's there?" I kept quite still and said nothing. For a whole hour I did not move a muscle, and in the meantime I did not hear him lie down. He was still sitting up in the bed listening—just as I have done, night after night, hearkening to the death watches in the wall.

Another question raised in such an account is whether we are to believe the narrator's description. Since he did not hear the man lie down, perhaps we are to assume that the old man did not lie down. Or perhaps we are to recognize that the narrator is experiencing lapses in memory, that perhaps we should not be convinced that the narrator is capable of truly narrating the story.

This passage also uses many comparisons to "Link[. . .] the notion of time with the beating of the old man's heart [which] connects with two other important motifs in the story: the title 'The Tell-Tale Heart,' and the narrator's identification with the old man" (May 76). In this way, the images of time not only add suspense to the story, but also create the love necessary for the shock of the murder. In "The Black Cat," this love was provided by the long-standing marriage of the narrator to his victim. May continues:

> If we ask what kind of tale the heart "tells" in this story we know that it does not "tell" in the usual metaphoric way; that is, we cannot look into the secret heart of the narrator to ascertain his motive. Instead, the tale the heart tells is linked to the beating of the heart being identified with time; that is, the tale the heart tells is the tale every heart tells: every beat marks an irretrievable moment in time that takes one closer to death. (May 76-77)

However, the narrator is overly cautious about the movements he makes and the exact moment he initiates another step towards the deed. One could say that as long as the narrator takes his time, the murder will go smoothly and he will go unpunished. The identification with the old man is completed at the moment of death by "the mournful influence of the unperceived shadow that caused him to feel—although he neither saw nor heard—to *feel* the presence of my head within the room."

In describing the murder, the narrator of "The Tell-Tale Heart" echoes the justification of the narrator of "The Black Cat": he was provoked. Only here, the narrator was provoked by the groan of the old man, rather than by the wails of a demonic cat, as the narrator tells of the murder in "The Tell-Tale Heart":

> Presently I heard a slight groan, and I knew it was the groan of mortal terror. It was not a groan of pain or of grief—oh, no!—it was the low stifled sound that arises from the bottom of the soul when overcharged with awe. I knew the sound well. Many a night, just at midnight, when all the world slept, it has welled up from my own bosom, deepening, with its dreadful echo, the terrors that distracted me. I say I knew it well. I knew what the old man felt, and pitied him, although I chuckled at heart.

Unlike "The Black Cat," this narrator seems to indicate some degree of sympathy. This sympathy confuses the reader: should we feel for the narrator because he pities the old man? Should we feel sorry for the narrator because he plainly suffers from a disorder that is maddening? Or should we feel angry with ourselves for judging the narrator as a cold-blooded murderer when, in fact, he is not responsible for his actions due to his mental condition? While the narrator of "The Black Cat" attempts to garner sympathy, this narrator more effectively carries out the call for empathy by directly admitting compassion.

The narrator of "The Tell-Tale Heart" continues to shift the reader's feelings as he justifies the reasons why the murder must take place. The old man should not have to suffer from the evils of the night; he should not be frightened anymore by noises after dark. The narrator can relate to the old man's groan and decides that he would be better off freed from the heinous world of darkness. Thus he kills the old man out of a sense of mercy (though the reader knows this mercy is deranged).

In the description of that which provoked the narrator to murder, we see the eye as we see the cat of "The Black Cat." The narrator uses the eye as a motive for murder. The eye "chilled his marrow;" therefore, he knew that the murder must take place soon. Each narrator feels justified in his murder. Further, each narrator defends his sanity. Here, the narrator addresses his own sanity: "And now have I not told you that what you mistake for madness is but over-acuteness of the senses?" As he unfolds the tale of murder, he not only indicates that the murder is justified, but also that he is trustworthy, more trustworthy, in fact, than the average person, for his senses are extraordinarily keen. For the reader, interpreting the narrator's keen sense involves focusing on the element of delusion in spite of precise logic. Yet here, even his logic seems to fall apart. He remains logical in carrying out the murder, but he makes illogical associations (like hearing the old man's heart from the next room).

As the narrator of "The Black Cat" obsesses over the cat, itself, and its meow, the narrator of "The Tell-Tale Heart" obsesses over the old man and his heartbeat; he even fears that the neighbors will hear the heart. Neither the entombment of the old man nor the entombment of the cat quells the sound created by the conscience of either narrator. In each, the reader eventually recognizes that the sound is a hallucination created by the mind of the narrator. The degree to which the sound is hallucination created by conscience permits the reader to interpret that this narrator is suffering from insanity.

As time runs out—the neighbors may hear the heartbeat—the narrator begins to lose composure as the narrator in "The Black Cat." However, in

"The Tell-Tale Heart" the narrator does not describe the actual murder. In "The Black Cat" the narrator murders his wife accidentally, and so the narrator can transfer his own guilt to the cat. However, in "The Tell-Tale Heart," since the old man never did anything to the narrator, the murder of the old man necessarily causes the narrator to feel guilty. To retain the proper poise for telling the rest of the story, the narrator omits the details of the heinous crime.

Just as in "The Black Cat," the narrator's sanity declines as his chances of his "getting away with it" increase. The narrator's speech and tone reveal his own sense of guilt, his lapse into insanity. The narrative seems to break into two different viewpoints, as the narrator's composure diminishes. Eventually, the narrator shows the officers in their satisfied state sitting at ease, while the narrator grows increasingly erratic as a result of the guilt.

III.

Sub conservatione formae specificae salva anima.

—*Raymond Lully*

I AM come of a race noted for vigor of fancy and ardor of passion. Men have called me mad; but the question is not yet settled, whether madness is or is not the loftiest intelligence— whether much that is glorious—whether all that is profound— does not spring from disease of thought—from *moods* of mind exalted at the expense of the general intellect. They who dream by day are cognizant of many things which escape those who dream only by night. In their gray visions they obtain glimpses of eternity, and thrill, in waking, to find that they have been upon the verge of the great secret.

The narrator in "Eleonora," a narrative exalting not only madness but also love in its most obsessive manner, follows the same pattern of madness as in "The Black Cat" and "The Tell-Tale Heart". The narrator begins the story by explaining that he has been called mad, but according to Poe's initial explanation, the narrator may simply be extremely intelligent. The first paragraph is placed strategically to add a plausible effect to the story about to be "penned." The narrator recognizes that some of his readers will find him mad, and some of his readers will justify the madness by the fact that he has fallen in love. The love that he speaks of later in the story is the kind that Charles May associates with obsession. May explains that:

> When one is obsessed, by definition, one's obsession becomes the center of one's experience and perception. As a result, everything the obsessed person experiences or perceives is transformed into an image of the obsession, and nothing is allowed to enter into the experiential framework of the person except those things that fit in with the obsession. (May 69)

Although May views this love as consuming, transforming all claims to the notion of obsession, the readers are open to many other fascinating interpretations concerning the narrator and his inner feelings. Certainly one interpretation of such an obsession is that of insanity. Following Prichard's criteria, one could deduce that the narrator suffers from hallucinogenic fits and can be considered morally insane.

As the narrator sets the tone for a struggle, he becomes torn between the spirit of his love and the reality of his life. Poe illustrates the struggle by using the repeated dashes, a trademark of his madness narratives, to force a feeling of anxiety upon the reader. The dashes are used a bit differently in "Eleonora" from the way they are used in "The Black Cat" and "The Tell-Tale Heart." In this story, the narrator places the dashes to separate phrases that attempt to add confusion to the validity of the narrator's claims.

The acclaimed "Am I mad" dilemma begins in the second paragraph of the tale, and rather than asking the rhetorical question (Am I mad?) or feigning sanity, the narrator openly declares his madness:

> We will say, then, that I am mad. I grant, at least, that there are two distinct conditions of my mental existence—the condition of a lucid reason, not to be disputed, and belonging to the memory of events forming the first epoch of my life—and a condition of shadow and doubt, appertaining to the present, and to the recollection of what constitutes the second great era of my being. Therefore, what I shall tell of the earlier period, believe; and to what I may relate of the later time, give only such credit as may seem due; or doubt it altogether; or, if doubt it yet cannot, then play unto its riddle the Oedipus.

Immediately, the narrator lays the groundwork to justify his questionable insanity. By convincing the reader to believe all that is said in the past (because that was a different life for him), the narrator validates his story. He admits that his present life may be tainted with the disease of madness to inform the reader that the narrator recognizes his own madness. In this, the narrator has empowered himself to define madness and its reasonable application. Because of this empowerment, the reader is likely to lend more credibility to the narrator. Paradoxically, because he is able to say that he currently has some mental doubt, we attribute to him the power of reasoning his own mental state.

The narrator further suggests that if we choose not to credit his story, then we can play with the riddle of Oedipus, a clue that the narrator is concerned with the aging of man. Richard Benton asserts that the narrator insinuates the riddle to deal specifically with "how the power of love operates during two important stages—namely, during adolescence and adulthood" (Benton 7). This assertion parallels the third paragraph in the story, "She whom I loved in youth, and of whom I now pen calmly and distinctly these remembrance . . . Eleonora was the name of my cousin." The narrator admits that time has passed and even so, he has his memories and can still "pen" calmly in her name:

> We had always dwelled together, beneath a tropical sun, in the Valley of the Many-Colored Grass. No unguided footstep ever came upon that vale; for it lay far away up among a range of giant hills that hung beetling around about it, shutting out the sunlight from its sweetest recesses. No path was trodden in its vicinity; and, to reach our happy home, there was need of putting back, with force, the foliage of many thousands of forest trees, and of crushing to death the glories of many millions of fragrant flowers.

In this passage the narrator casts doubt to his sanity by describing his home as a carbon copy of a fairytale castle or a Shakespearean magical realm (like the Forest of Arden). Even though the narrator claims that this land exists in his first era of life, the reader has to question the validity of the narrator's "magical" world.

In the next three paragraphs, the narrator seems to be serene as he describes the possible incestuous relationship turning into a partnership full of vibrancy and power. The partnership is foreshadowed by the narrator's choice of natural surroundings. For example, the narrator and his "love" walk along a river that flows into a mountain that is "carpeted by soft green grass, thick, short, perfectly even, and vanilla-perfumed, [and also] besprinkled throughout with the yellow buttercup, the white daisy, the purple violet, and the ruby-red asphodel. . . ." The wide variety of flowers and colors are used to personify the love that is about to transpire. Nature is viewed as the "land of innocence" (Weigel 58), manipulating the reader into believing that because the relationship is formed in nirvana, the narrator cannot possibly be considered mad.

By mentioning the spirit of the god that represented the "creative principle of attraction that brings beings together, establishes friendships and marriages," (Weigel 43) the narrator claims that he and Eleonora are possessed by the power of the god Eros, drawn from

> that wave, and now we felt that he had enkindled within us the fiery souls of our forefathers. The passions which had for centuries distinguished our race, came thronging with the fancies for which they had been equally noted, and together breathed a delirious bliss over the Valley of the Many-Colored Grass.

Again, the narrator slips into a world of enchantment, leaving his readers to distinguish whether his claim of previous sanity is sound. Another possible interpretation for the need to have Eros as a guide through the "wave" is the need for the narrator to cover his own feeling of guilt. The guilt is driven by the fact that the narrator is nearly five years older than Eleonora, and in spite of the age difference, he continues with the relationship although it is likely incestuous.

The following transformation that the narrator describes is enough evidence to negate the sanity claim and add to the proposed interpretation of guilt. He says, "[a] change fell upon all things. Strange, brilliant flowers, star-shaped, burst out upon the trees where no flowers had been known before." Considering that the entire page deals with this fairytale-like enchanted change, the narrator appears insane in the reader's eyes. The change can be viewed in two fundamentally different ways. In the first, the narrator is insane because the changes that he describes are imaginary. Flowers do not grow out of trees that have never blossomed before, and numerous flowers do not grow in place of one, especially a different type of flower. Perhaps the narrator is obsessing over the guilt he feels because he is the cause of the fall of his "cousin's" innocence. In the second way, the narrator's change is morbid. The narrator is still to be considered insane, but perhaps Prichard would assert he drove himself insane because he is, in fact, the reason for his Eleonora's death. He could be viewed as the murderer. After all, the narrator never reveals the cause of his love's death. In fact, he says that if he breaks his promise of eternal fidelity to her, a penalty " . . .the exceeding great horror of which will not permit [him] to make record of. . . ." will be placed on him.

The fact that he *cannot* share with his reader the cause of his love's death indicates his potential underlying guilt. Obviously something has taken residence in his mind; this view asserts that it is guilt or the madness inflicted by guilt.

The narrator attempts to strengthen the claim that his past is believable by shifting the notion of spiritual reincarnation on to his dying lover. He states:

> And she said to me, not many days afterward, tranquilly dying, that, because of what I had done for the comfort of her spirit she would watch over me in that spirit when departed, and, if so it were permitted her return to me visibly in the watches of the night; but, if this thing were, indeed, beyond the power of the souls in Paradise, that she would, at least, give me frequent indications of her presence; sighing upon me in the evening winds, or filling the air which I breathed with perfume from the censers of the angels. And, with these words upon her lips, she yielded up her innocent life, putting an end to the first epoch of my own.

The notion that Eleonora will come back to "haunt" the narrator is a form of supernaturalism. Since we cannot account for the truth of such acts, we can characterize the thought as plausible. There are no explained phenomena recorded in history to give validation to Eleonora's claim; therefore, the reader can assume that the narrator is playing "mind games" (Honer 61-62). The reader may also assume, as an alternative theory, that the narrator believes that Eleonora's spirit is actually haunting him; hence he is insane. The narrator puts an end to the first "epoch of [his] life," leaving his reader with the feeling of anxiety:

> Thus far I have faithfully said. But as I pass the barrier in Time's path, formed by the death of my beloved, and proceed with the second era of my existence, I feel that a shadow gathers over my brain, and I mistrust the perfect sanity of the record. But let me on—.

The shadow the narrator refers to is the hazy lingering of guilt. Here Poe plays with his reader by illustrating the narrator's distrust of his very own sanity. How are we to believe the narrator is telling us a true story if he, himself, does not know whether he is insane? Perhaps this is another way that Poe draws his readers into his work so that we can begin to question what we have read thus far.

Another example of Poe's continuing parallel with images found in his other tales is Eleonora's death, which can be compared to time's path. The death/path symbolizes the anxiety that grows within the narrators' minds because of the maddening acts that they so cruelly avoid. In "The Tell-Tale Heart," time is a recurring symbol of the security to which the narrator clings. Time is the only friend the narrator has in all three of these stories. The narrators feel they can accomplish anything as long as they take their time and think their actions out completely. In "Eleonora" the narrator views time as his savior concerning his promise that he made either in love, or in an attempt to absolve himself for the murder of "his angel." This insistence upon "taking time" as a savior illustrates qualities of an obsessed person.

Unlike the other two tales, the narrator questions his own sanity. Part of his questioning results from the unbelievable scenery at the beginning of the tale. The narrator tells his reader that through the passing of time the land of enchantment has died. The flowers have died, and the stream has turned back into the stream of Silence, leaving the narrator to doubt his captivated past in the Valley of the Many-Colored Grass. Further, he relates that he never forgot Eleonora, for

> I heard the sounds of the swinging of the censers of the angels; and streams of a holy perfume floated ever and ever about the valley; and at lone hours, when my heart beat heavily, the winds that bathed my brow came unto me laden with soft sighs; and indistinct murmurs filled often the night air; and once—oh, but once only! I was awakened from a slumber, like the slumber of death, by the pressing of spiritual lips upon my own.

But perhaps the primary cause of his questioning is the mysterious death of his Eleonora. "The Black Cat" and "The Tell-Tale Heart" indicate the effects of unpunished evil, the madness caused by the unavenged death of an innocent. For when the narrator encounters the spirit of Eleonora he says that he was awakened from a slumber of death, which means that he was sleeping as soundly as a corpse when tucked away in *her* coffin. Since the narrator says that he himself does not believe the second era of his life, so we should not either, yet it seems that the possibility of belief is more acceptable in this part of his life. His description is believable and his actions are more acceptable than in the earlier part of the tale, perhaps because he sets this description as a dream. This recognition of the difference between dream and reality permits the reader to identify with the narrator. It is also possible that the narrator is suffering from a guilty conscience and needs to feel that Eleonora still loves him even though he murdered her. For his own self-assurance, he imagines that she visits him. With this "visit" the narrator feels the loss (or guilt) for Eleonora and must leave the valley forever. Finding himself in a strange city where he can attempt to make a new life for himself, the narrator continues to feel committed to his promise, as his soul

> had proved true to its vows, and the indications of the presence of Eleonora were still given me in the silent hours of the night. Suddenly these manifestations they ceased, and the world grew dark before mine eyes, and I stood aghast at the burning thoughts which possessed, at the terrible temptations which beset me. . .

The narrator makes a complete turn around in his life, not only in location but in his personal choices as well. Fleeing the valley, the narrator wishes to put his past behind him and start over, but not once does he say that he wishes to find another love. He only insinuates a possible future love by sharing his loneliness with us. He says, "I longed for the love which had before filled it [his heart] to overflowing." Later, the narrator meets a maiden whom he feels is the "light of his life," so to speak. In referring to her, he states, "Oh, bright was the seraph Ermengarde!" which indicates his infatuation with her. He is so infatuated that he marries her, breaking his vow to Eleonora. He never thinks about the dreaded curse, ". . . I had no room for none other. . . . I thought only of them [Ermengarde's eyes] —and of *her*." Remembering that we are in the second era of the narrator's life, we question the validity of what he presents to us. The "her" in this line likely refers to Eleonora. The narrator's repression of guilt from his first epoch of life, whether it be because of the age difference/incest or because he actually murdered his cousin/lover, could be tainting his new life. The narrator could be imagining the entire second era of his life. He tells us: "What I may relate of the later time, give only such credit as may seem due. . . ." It is possible that he killed his cousin and that the guilt from murder drove him insane, leading to the imaginative second era of the tale. Being aware of his possible insanity, the narrator personifies freedom and invests his independence in Ermengarde. If Ermengarde is a personification of the narrator's desire to feel secure, then the story seems as if it is one big confessional. His absolution has been granted only in his own mind in order to live with the consequences of his youth; the narrator derives the illusion that his first lover comes back from the dead to forgive him:

> Sleep in peace! For thy Spirit of Love reigneth and ruleth, and, in taking to thy passionate heart her who is Ermengarde, thou art

absolved, for reasons which shall be made known to thee in
Heaven, of thy vows unto Eleonora.

Again, the ambiguity of madness and the symbols of uncertainty leave Poe's
reader with a feeling of obscurity. In "The Black Cat," the confusion centers
on the cat itself. In "The Tell-Tale Heart," the beating of the heart causes
duplicity, and in "Eleonora," the ambivalence can be attributed to the image
of the ghost. With these rhetorical devices, Poe is able to keep his reader
guessing about the reliability of his narrators.

In reviewing Poe's very own epistemology on madness as well as his
criteria for evaluating a talented writer, which plays a large part in
determining whether Poe's narrators are indeed, trustworthy, and by
understanding Poe's idea of monomania in connection with his discussion of
talent stemming from the genius that is the direct result of madness, we have
a foundation for analyzing Poe's fiction. To add to this foundation, it is
necessary to be aware of the possibility that Poe may use outrageous plots,
bizarre character names, and paradoxical statements to undermine narrator
credibility and reader stability. In Poe's own words:

> [I]n a case where mental power is inordinately great, [it] gives
> that result which *is* the true *genius* (but which, on account of the
> proportion and seemingly simplicity of its works, is seldom
> acknowledged to *be* so;) and the genius is greater or less, first, as
> the general mental power is more or less inordinately great; and,
> secondly, as the proportion of the faculties is more or less
> absolute. (Foye 38)

While he contradicts his very own thoughts from one paragraph to the
next, he twists his words to make perfect sense to the ambitious critic who
has the foundation to analyze Poe's writing. To interrogate the above ideas
from Poe's essay would be a process by which Poe, himself, would look at and
feel satisfied, for he displays an evident paradox in his writing. To answer the
question as to whether a genuinely mad person is capable of asking the
question "Am I mad?" would be a movement against Poe's own philosophy.

According to Poe's idea of mental power, that which is "inordinately
great . . . is genius" (Foye 38), and genius is seldom ever recognized for its
true faculties that stem from the overlooked simplicity of work, an oversight
on the part of the critic. To ignore Poe's motives for tricking his readers
would be to ignore his own genius. Since genius is rooted in intellect, and
talent is evaluated by the level of the writer's intellect, we can assume Poe
viewed himself as a "genius." Poe states that the greatest excess of mental

power "does not seem to satisfy our [critics] idea of genius, unless we have, in addition, sensibility, passion, [and] energy" (Foye 38). To embody all of these things is to be a genuine genius in the eyes of the critic. Although Poe was sometimes negated by his contemporaries, he remained certain that he was, indeed, one who possessed these genius characteristics. To read Poe's fiction with this in mind is to know that Poe considered himself to be of the "loftiest intelligence," one who could present the question of madness in his tale, but negate the claim of being mad by contradicting the insanity theme with "sensibility, passion, and energy" (Foye 38). It is these three characteristics that create the instability of the reader in Poe's fiction and at the same time draw the reader further into the story to experience the mystery he pens.

Works Cited

Benton, Richard. *Bedlam Patterns: Love and the Idea of Madness in Poe's Fiction.* Baltimore: Edgar Allan Poe Society, 1979.

The Complete Tales & Poems of Edgar Allan Poe. New York: Vintage Books Edition, September 1975.

Foye, Raymond ed. *The Unknown Poe.* San Francisco: City Lights Books, 1980.

Halliburton, David. *Edgar Allan Poe: A Phenomenological View.* New York: Princeton University Press, 1973.

Honer, Stanley M. *Invitation to Philosophy: Issues and Options.* New York: Wadsworth Publishing Company, 1996.

May, Charles L. *Edgar Allan Poe: A Study of the Short Fiction*, Boston: Twayne Publishers, 1991.

Meinsma, Robert. "A Brief History of Mental Therapy." online. 10 Jun. 2001.
<http://home.earthlink.net/~openbook/History.mental.therapy.html>

Peeples, Scott. *Edgar Allan Poe Revisited.* New York: Twayne Publishers, 1998.

Rosen, George. *Madness in Society: Chapters in the Historical Sociology of Mental Illness.* London: Rortledge & Kegan Paul, 1968.

Weigel, James Jr., M.A. *Mythology.* Nebraska: C. K. Hillegass, 1991.

JOHN CLEMAN

Irresistible Impulses: Edgar Allan Poe and the Insanity Defense

Poe's fascination with stories of crime, sometimes gleaned from contemporary newspaper accounts, is obvious enough from such examples as "The Oblong Box" (1844), "The Mystery of Marie Rogét" (1842–43), and "The Murders in the Rue Morgue" (1841). In these and similar tales Poe's interest centers on the processes of detection, leaving the moral issues of the crimes either largely unaddressed or curiously deflected. "The Murders in the Rue Morgue" presents a rather stark version of this formulation. The crime solved turns out to be no crime at all: the fiend who brutally kills and mutilates an innocent mother and daughter is an orang-utan, and neither the beast nor its owner can be held morally responsible. Furthermore, this stripping of moral content seems a purposeful irony or tantalization. The processes of social and legal justice, apparently set in motion by the detective work of both the police and Auguste Dupin, lead to a blank or dissolution where the presumptions of human agency are blurred into an image of instinctive brutality.

Such a treatment can be seen as part of an apparent lack of interest in moral themes throughout Poe's work. As Stuart Levine observes, "It is fair to say that in most of his stories which raise moral issues, Poe's concern is focused elsewhere."[1] To some degree, this seeming indifference to moral issues can be explained by Poe's aesthetic in which the "Moral Sense," "Conscience," and "Duty" have, at best, "only collateral relations" with the

From *American Literature*, Vol. 63, no. 4, December 1991. © 1991 by Duke University Press.

primary concerns: for poetry *"The Rhythmical Creation of Beauty,"*[2] and for prose fiction "the unity of effect or impression."[3] Apart from the aesthetic, Poe's emphasis is usually read to center in the psychological or in the exercise of an individual will acting as a microcosm of the Universal Will. Edward Davidson, for example, observes that "Poe removed all moral and religious considerations as far as possible from any social code or body of religious warrants." Operating in a universe in which there is "no other god but the self as god,"[4] each of the characters "in Poe's moral inquiries is his own moral arbiter, lodged in a total moral anarchy. Society has invented law and justice, but these are mere illusion and exact no true penalty."[5] Similarly, Vincent Buranelli insists, "Poe does not touch morality. Although his aesthetic theory admits that goodness may be a by-product of art, he himself does not look for it. Sin and crime are absent from this part of the universe; and the terrible deeds that abound there are matters of psychology, not of ethics."[6]

Davidson's and Buranelli's readings, characteristic of the general tendency to view Poe's fiction as largely divorced from the social and historical context in which he wrote, pose a particular problem for stories of crime such as "The Murders in the Rue Morgue," especially when the stories center in the mind of the criminal. "Matters of psychology" are inescapably relevant to the formulation of the *mens rea* and, therefore, are crucial to the definition of acts as crimes. Thus, to deflect the significance of a crime from the social and moral to the psychological has a specific social and legal meaning, most apparent in the instance of an insanity defense. Such deflections, in fact, were a significant part of a controversy over the use of the insanity defense in the first half of the nineteenth century, particularly in the early 1840s. Three stories from this period—"The Tell-Tale Heart" (1843), "The Black Cat" (1843), and "The Imp of the Perverse" (1845)—especially invite a reading in the context of the insanity-defense controversy because each of the three tales includes a self-defensive, insane murderer whose story is told within the processes of legal justice.[7] The stories suggest that Poe's narrowed focus on the aberrant psychology of the accused criminal, for whatever it owes to his aesthetic theory, general "otherworldliness," and private demons, also has a locus in specific jurisprudential issues of his day.

In England, the controversy over the increased use of the insanity defense in the first half of the nineteenth century was stimulated by a number of factors.[8] The political nature of the most celebrated cases, especially that of Daniel McNaughton in 1843, argued to many that the defense was undermining civil order.[9] In addition, asylum reform and the increased popularity of what was known as "moral treatment" of the insane certainly contributed to the public perception that to be acquitted on the basis of insanity was to avoid punishment. Through most of the two centuries prior to Pinel's celebrated unchaining of several mentally ill patients at Bicêtre in 1793, the insane were treated very much like criminals, often locked up together in the same prisons, subjected to similar restraints and corporal punishments short of execution.[10] With the reforms, the insane were housed apart from criminals and, to some degree, treated with the compassion and care afforded the physically ill.[11] Finally, there was an increased use of medical testimony in court to determine insanity, corresponding to a broader movement to establish the study of the mind on a scientific basis. This testimony not only presented a strongly deterministic view of human nature; it also described as insane, and therefore not culpable, individuals who gave every appearance of rationality.

Poe's familiarity with the scientific/medical accounts of insanity of his day has been well established,[12] and his awareness of the issues of the insanity-defense controversy can be linked to two specific cases in which the defense was employed, both occurring in the environs of Philadelphia where Poe resided between 1838 and 1844, and both featuring the same attorney, Peter A. Browne, who "had distinguished himself . . . for his great subtilty and deep metaphysical research in the matter of *insanity*."[13] In the first of these, James Wood was acquitted on the grounds of insanity of the deliberate murder of his daughter. Lengthy accounts of the trial appeared daily in the Philadelphia *Public Ledger* from 24 to 30 March 1840, and a comment at its conclusion appearing in the 1 April 1840 issue of *Alexander's Weekly Messenger* has been attributed to Poe.[14]

The second case, the trial of Singleton Mercer, while less directly linked to Poe, signals more clearly the terms of the insanity-defense controversy. Mercer was charged with murdering his sister's seducer in February 1843. Both Mercer and his victim were well-known "men about town"[15] in Philadelphia, and the Philadelphia and New York newspapers carried daily accounts of the court's proceedings, loaded with sensational details of sex, violence, and public corruption.[16] Poe's friend and lifelong supporter George Lippard made direct use of the case in his best-selling novel *Quaker City, or The Monks of Monk Hall* (1844). The fact that a later stage version was banned in Philadelphia out of fear that the attendance of Mercer and his supporters would cause a riot suggests that the case had a long, prominent life in the consciousness of Philadelphians.[17] In short, the Mercer trial was a major part of Philadelphia public life from 1843 to 1845, and it is nearly impossible to imagine Poe not being aware of it.

The importance of the Mercer case for Poe's fiction, however, may be less its notoriety and lurid details than the fact that insanity was made the primary grounds of defense.[18] A complete transcript of Browne's opening remarks on the defense was printed on the front page of the 31 March 1843 issue of the Philadelphia *Public Ledger*. In light of the likelihood that Poe read them, Browne's arguments are interesting and significant because they include a fairly thorough synopsis of the main legal, medical, and philosophical issues underlying the insanity defense. They also reflect the terms of the controversy surrounding its increased use. Thus, at the very least, Browne's remarks provide a window on the public consciousness of the insanity defense—for both Poe and his readers—during the time in which "The Tell-Tale Heart," "The Black Cat," and "The Imp of the Perverse" were written and published.[19]

Several features of Browne's insanity-defense argument have particular significance as a backdrop to the three stories we are considering. In the first place, he begins by directly acknowledging the controversy over the use of the defense. He admits that the defense "has of late become an object of ridicule," in part because it "has been abused, by relying upon it where none [no insanity] existed." He also acknowledges that some may find the ideas supporting his arguments to be either "'new fangled doctrines'" or, even worse, a "*modern French* notion." His first task, therefore, is to establish the legitimacy of the defense itself, and to do so he will need not only to cite legal principle and precedent but also to undermine the popular suspicion that the concept of the defense is a foreign and speciously sophisticated intrusion into the American world of common sense and plain Christian morality.

More significantly, Browne focuses on partial insanity or monomania as the central issue inviting controversy. With regard to the general use of the insanity defense it is enough for him simply to assert, "In all civilized countries, ancient and modern, insanity has been regarded as exempting from punishment." The problem was that up to the end of the eighteenth century the most common test of exculpatory insanity rooted in Christian morality was "the knowledge of good and evil."[20] The equation between reason and the moral sense was nearly absolute, and therefore any sign of rationality—such as appearing calm and reasonable in court, premeditating or planning the crime, or seeking to hide or avoid punishment—demonstrated the presence of an indivisible conscience and concomitant moral responsibility. Thus, to qualify for legal exemption, the mentally defective individual needed to be, in the well-known opinion of one eighteenth-century judge, "a man that is totally deprived of his understanding and memory, and doth not know what he is doing, no more than an infant, than a brute, or a wild beast."[21] Few qualified under this "wild beast" test, and those that did met commonsense, obvious-perception standards of madness. However, as the courts in the nineteenth century began increasingly to accept arguments for an exculpatory *partial* insanity, more qualified for the defense, its use increased, and the accused frequently no longer fit the obvious, commonsense image of insanity. Hence, in large part, the controversy.

Browne cites numerous legal and medical authorities, mostly from the late eighteenth century on, to demonstrate that the equation between rationality and moral responsibility is not absolute. An individual may display considerable powers of intellect on a wide range of subjects, including the planning and execution of his crime, and still not be responsible for his actions. Even the knowledge of good and evil, he insists, is an inadequate test of insanity, for it does not answer the crucial question, whether or not the accused was "incapable of exercising free will." For Browne, the only test of exculpable lunacy is fairly clean-cut: "A lunatic is one 'WHO HAS LOST THE USE OF HIS REASON,'" not totally lost or "deprived of his reason" but "one 'who hath lost the USE of his reason,' which includes those who still having intellect cannot use it, because either their affections or their will are deranged."[22]

A third point suggesting links to Poe is Browne's use of Dr. Isaac Ray, America's leading nineteenth-century authority on medical jurisprudence, cited in the McNaughton trial and best known, perhaps, for developing the theory of "irresistible impulse," a form of "moral insanity." What is interesting here is that his central concept of the human mind—hence the basis of his medical jurisprudence—was grounded in the phrenological theories of Gall and Spurzheim. Ray argued that the moral (affective) and rational (intellectual) functions of the brain were physically separate, located in different mental organs and each independently susceptible to disease and deformation. Thus, an individual suffering a disease of the moral organs could become a victim of "moral insanity" in which "no *delusion* is present to disturb the mental vision" and yet he "finds himself urged, perhaps, to the commission of every outrage, and though perfectly conscious of what he is doing, unable to offer the slightest resistance to the overwhelming power that impels him."[23] To illustrate this, Ray recounts the cases of a number of homicidal maniacs and then concludes that "they all possess one feature in common, the *irresistible, motiveless impulse to destroy life.*"[24]

By the time of Ray's *Treatise*, however, phrenology had become a disreputable science, not only because of the quackery of many of its bump-reading practitioners but also because it had long been recognized as irreligious. Furthermore, when phrenology was employed in insanity-defense cases, conservative legal authorities objected that it provided an argument for excusing all criminal behavior as the result of diseased mental organs. Thus, to one of Ray's leading opponents in the 1850s and 1860s the phrenologically based concept of moral insanity was merely "another name for depravity," a sign of chaotic nature.[25] In writing his *Treatise* Ray consciously sought to play down and hide overt references to phrenology, but the work offered, nevertheless, an essentially deterministic view of the human mind.[26]

Thus, the insanity-defense arguments of the mid-nineteenth century—those such as Browne's which helped provoke the controversy—posited a view of human nature ruled not by reasoned choice but by chance and ultimately mysterious physical forces. Not only was the boundary between the rational and irrational blurred, often wearing the same mask, the grounds for moral responsibility shifted as well. As Browne observed, courts and the public were asked to change their opinion "as to [the] *real nature of actions*, which are either *atrocious crimes*, or the *dreadful effects of disease*."[27] The signalling feature to effect this shift from condemnation to pity was an inexplicable compulsion, an impelling force potential in everyone.

Of the three tales we are considering, "The Tell-Tale Heart" presents the most apparent evidence of Poe's use of the issues of the insanity defense. The characteristic form of all three tales is not confession but self-defense, an attempt to provide a rational account of apparently irrational events and behavior. In "The Tell-Tale Heart" there is a good deal of dramatic immediacy to this defense. The narrator addresses a specific but unnamed "you" sometime after his arrest but obviously before his execution (if there is to be one). His aim is to refute "you" 's claim that he is insane, a charge that has apparently been both specific and formal enough for the narrator to feel the necessity of responding in earnest and in detail. From the abrupt opening ("True!—nervous—very, very dreadfully nervous I had been and am: but why *will* you say that I am mad?") to the final dramatic breakdown ("and now—again!—hark! louder! louder! louder! *louder!*") the narration seems more spoken than written, something like a courtroom outburst or final statement of the accused.[28]

The point of suggesting such a context for the tale's telling is to underscore a particular significance of the narrator's insistence on his own sanity. The argument he offers reflects the issues of the insanity-defense controversy, both in the way he measures his own state of mind and in the type of madman he reveals himself to be. His argument echoes the terms by which an eighteenth-century prosecutor, employing the "wild beast" test of insanity, might have differentiated the accused (himself) from the recognizably nonculpable madman. Such madmen, according to the narrator, are mentally defective ("Madmen know nothing"), physically impaired ("senses...destroyed...dulled"), incapable of wisdom or "sagacity" (pp. 792–93) in planning, at the mercy of impulse and passion. He, on the other hand, exhibited unmistakable signs of rational behavior in the way he carried out his crime: note, he repeatedly insists, "how wisely I proceeded—with what caution—with what foresight." He also asks the auditor to "observe how healthily—how calmly" he "can tell you the whole story." Thus, insofar as the narrator is manifestly not a "wild beast," the "prosecutor's argument" succeeds: the narrator is capable of reason and is, therefore, morally and legally responsible for his acts.

Of course, in telling his tale, particularly if imagined as a statement in court, the narrator is also offering clear evidence that he is by contemporary standards partially insane. Like the many monomaniacs Browne describes, the narrator has a highly developed intellect, is capable of planning and remembering his actions in great detail, but his intellect and energies are fixed unreasonably on a single goal or "one dominant idea" (the old man's "vulture eye") "that rides rough-shod over his brain—that haunts him day and night until it is granted."[29] Elizabeth Phillips has demonstrated that the narrator resembles the homicidal maniacs described by Ray and Rush in several respects, including his singular lack of rational motive, his unusual cruelty, his remaining at the scene of the crime, his symptoms of delusions and hallucinations, and his acuteness of the senses, headaches, and ringing in the ears.[30] However, the most convincing proof of his insanity seems to be the very mask of sanity he purports to wear. Ray argued that "madness is not indicated so much by any particular extravagance of thought or feeling, as by a well-marked change of character or departure from the ordinary habits of thinking, feeling and acting, without any adequate external cause."[31] Thus, the narrator's calmness, deliberateness, and rationality signal insanity insofar as they are at variance with his "normal" state ("very, very dreadfully nervous I had been and am"), particularly as that is revealed in the frenetic last few paragraphs. Even the narrator's insistent denial of the charge of insanity fits the pattern of symptoms of the homicidal maniac, so that the act of the tale's telling and its self-defensive posture constitute evidence in a determination of partial insanity.[32]

The irony of ostensible sanity signaling insanity could not have been lost on Poe, for this parallels his point in "The Trial of James Wood." Poe does not question Wood's acquittal but believes that the defense "omitted... an argument which, with many minds, would have had more weight in bringing about a conviction of the prisoner's insanity than any urged in his behalf." Poe reasons that Wood's calm, rational deliberation when he purchased the pistols used to kill his daughter, the signs that, "upon a cursory view . . . do certainly make against the accused, and imply a premeditated and cold-blooded assassination," are the clear signs of insanity "to the metaphysician, or the skilful medical man." Following Ray, the specific basis for this claim is that Wood's "remarkable calmness" was at variance with "his usual nervous habit" and the "cause for agitation which he is known to have had." More generally, Poe extols "the cunning of the maniac—a cunning which baffles that of the wisest man of sound mind—the amazing self-possession with which at times, he assumes the demeanor, and preserves the appearance, of perfect sanity."[33]

Brigham and Mabbott may be right in suggesting the Poe drew on the James Wood trial in writing "The Tell-Tale Heart," but if so, the important points are Poe's fascination with rational behavior as evidence "bringing about a conviction of . . . insanity"[34] and his awareness of the consequences of that determination. Poe points out that Wood's acquittal "on the ground of insanity" meant his "legal confinement as a madman until such time as the Court satisfy themselves of his return to sound mind," a time Poe believes and hopes will never come: "His monomania is essentially periodical; and a perfect sanity for months, or even years, would scarcely be a sufficient guaranty for his subsequent conduct. A time would still come when there would be laid to his charge another—although hardly a more horrible—deed of sudden violence and bloodshed."[35] In light of this concern, Poe's interest in the "cunning of the maniac" in simulating "perfect sanity" has more than clinical or literary significance: properly recognized it may convict the accused of insanity, but it thereby acquits him of murder and offers the possibility of his ultimate release to murder again.

In "The Tell-Tale Heart" the outcome is less certain, but the same concerns seem to apply. If the narrator demonstrates his own insanity paralleling the homicidal mania evidenced by Wood, then the telling of the tale would seem to lead to acquittal and to an uneasily indeterminate incarceration. In this light, the death wish many critics have described as the essence of the narrator's compulsions to crime and confession would seem to be thwarted or deflected.[36] But, if the evidence of the narrator's insanity seems clear, it is difficult to read the story with the sense that he is exonerated because of it: the recognition of his madness does not convert his condemnable "*atrocious crimes*" to pitiable "*effects of disease.*" This may be due in part to the pride and arrogance of the narrator's intellect. It is due even more to the way the elements of the madness figure in the acts themselves. If, as Browne insists, the key test of exculpable insanity is the loss of the "USE" of reason, the most mysterious, unreasoned, and irresistible act in the story is the act of confession. In this way, Poe inverts or re-deflects the central argument of the insanity defense so that compulsion accounts not for the crime but for the crime and its perpetrator.

The pattern of the narrator seeking to defend his rationality but revealing instead his partial insanity is replicated in "The Black Cat." In this case, the issue of a charge of insanity is more oblique and subtle. It is suggested initially by the "indeed" in his opening observation: "For the most wild, yet most homely narrative which I am about to pen, I neither expect nor solicit belief. Mad indeed would I be to expect it." The implication of this seems to be that some have thought him mad, either for his acts or, perhaps, for his babblings about a persecuting demon cat. Or, at least, by laying his account of events before the bar of reason he is inviting the charge of insanity. Like the narrator of "The Tell-Tale Heart," he is self-conscious of the imputation that something either in the nature of the events he recounts or in the manner of his relating them will signal mental imbalance. Thus, he describes his narrative as "mere household events" (p. 849) that have "presented little but Horror" to him but "to many . . . will seem less terrible than *baroques*" (p. 850). "Here-after," he hopes, "some intellect may be found which will reduce my phantasm to the common-place—some intellect more calm, logical, and far less excitable than my own, which will perceive, in the circumstances I detail with awe, nothing more than an ordinary succession of very natural causes and effects."

In "The Black Cat" this attempt at rational explanation also reveals a pattern of madness that in certain respects parallels the monomania in "The Tell-Tale Heart." In the narrator's perception of the images of a cat on the wall of the burnt house and of a gallows on the breast of Pluto's successor, both of which he interprets as signs of a demonic persecution, we may recognize elements of delusion. His increasingly obsessive fear and hatred of the cats is also, like "The Tell-Tale Heart" narrator's excess of rational planning, a motiveless distortion and perversion of what might seem an otherwise healthy human impulse, his special fondness for animals. It is important to recognize the terms of this distortion, for while the narrator's criminal behavior may be blamed on "the Fiend Intemperance," a case of *mania a potu*,[37] the primary agents of his criminal fate were part of his nature, an excess of his distinguishing virtues: as he asserts, "From my infancy I was noted for the docility and humanity of my disposition. My tenderness of heart was even so conspicuous as to make me the jest of my companions." Whether or not because of this teasing, he indicates that he became "especially fond of animals," devoted most of his time to his pets, and "never was so happy as when feeding and caressing them." What is clearly a preference for animal over human companionship; he says, "grew with my growth, and, in my manhood, I derived from it one of my principal sources of pleasure." That this preference is in some degree *anti*-human can be recognized in his assertion, "There is something in the unselfish self-sacrificing love of a brute, which goes directly to the heart of him who has had frequent occasion to test the paltry friendship and gossamer fidelity of mere *Man*" (p. 850).

Clearly there is an imbalance in the narrator's makeup. His exceptional sweetness can find a reciprocating perfection of fidelity and kindness only in the mindless devotion of animals. Although no "wild beast" himself, the narrator ironically exhibits his monomania in attributing the values of both good and evil to the bestial. It is in this regard that the play of issues recognizable in the insanity-defense controversy becomes particularly interesting. The narrator, by his own account, is driven to his crimes by an irrational compulsion which he calls "the spirit of PERVERSENESS." This spirit, "one of the primitive impulses of the human heart—one of the indivisible primary faculties, or sentiments, which give direction to the character of Man," is defined as a principle of negation, the "unfathomable longing of the soul *to vex itself*—to offer violence to its own nature—to do wrong for the wrong's sake only." That this "irresistible impulse" has nullified his will against the dictates of a still viable conscience is manifest when he hangs Pluto, as he says, "*because* I knew that it had loved me, and *because* I felt it had given me no reason of offence;—hung it *because* I knew that in so doing I was committing a sin—a deadly sin that would so jeopardize my immortal soul as to place it—if such a thing were possible— even beyond the infinite mercy of the Most Merciful and Most Terrible God" (p. 852).

On these grounds we might recognize an exculpatory partial insanity, but as in the case of "The Tell-Tale Heart," the effect is other. Just as the narrator locates his early inordinate kindness in the love of animals, his explanation of perverseness locates an aspect of moral behavior in the irrational innocence of compulsion. It should be remembered that the concept of mind underlying the shift from a "wild beast" test of insanity to a test recognizing an exculpable partial insanity widened the domain of the bestial by widening the range of innocence. As if to expose this expansion, Poe develops the play of good and evil, of reason and madness, all centering on the animal, the cat: object, agent, and emblem. It is killing the cat that torments the narrator's conscience, that makes him believe he is beyond God's mercy. By contrast, when he kills his wife he shows almost no signs of remorse. He sets forth "with entire deliberation" to hide her body, and when he believes that concealment safely accomplished and the cat has fled the premises, he admits, "The guilt of my dark deed disturbed me but little" (p. 858). It is the first cat's innocence that drives him perversely to murder the beast, and with its unconscious markings it is the second cat that prefigures his fate and goads him to meet it. As agent of the narrator's fate and chief emblem of his monomania, the cat is to him "the hideous beast, whose craft had seduced me into murder, and whose informing voice had consigned me to the hangman" (p. 859).

Thus, in "The Black Cat" Poe would seem again to undermine the insanity-defense argument in several ways. Paralleling the pattern in "The

Tell-Tale Heart," the moral insanity of the narrator, the derangement of the affections that leads him to murder his wife out of a deflected rage against a cat, becomes in the figure of that cat the means to his exposure and punishment, the agent not of exculpation but of a kind of poetic justice. Furthermore, the arguments that locate all the terms of good and evil in the "*brute beast*" (p. 856) are the self-serving rationalizations of a madman. This is even more interestingly the case with the concept of "perverseness," which, like the arguments of Ray and other medical authorities, is presented as a logical, "philosophical" explanation that voids overtly immoral acts of their moral implications.

The sense in which perverseness ironically echoes the moral terms of the insanity-defense arguments and achieves a form of justice is presented more clearly, albeit more intricately, in "The Imp of the Perverse." The structure of the narrative resembles the patterns of the other two stories in that the narrator's overt aim is to make the apparently unreasonable reasonable, to ground the irrational in reason and logic. As in "The Tell-Tale Heart," the narrator addresses a "you," an unnamed second-person auditor/reader. He hopes to "assign to you something that shall have at least the faint aspect of a cause for" his "wearing these fetters, and . . . tenanting this cell of the condemned," so that "you" will not misunderstand him or "with the rabble" (pp. 1223–24) fancy him mad. The "cause" he refers to is perverseness, and the theory of mind that he uses to account for it is phrenology. One significance of the narrator's use of phrenology is that the allusion to the scientific/medical underpinnings for the insanity defense, perhaps implicit in "The Black Cat,"[38] is made fairly specific in "The Imp of the Perverse." This allusion seems underscored by the narrator's distinction between perverseness and a "modification of that which ordinarily springs from the *combativeness* of phrenology" (p. 1221), for it was precisely accounts of such modifications, caused by childhood diseases or head injuries, that phrenologists used to explain how criminal actions were the result of mental illness. Pointedly and ironically, in "The Imp of the Perverse" the narrator's phrenological, analysis argues for a healthy, "normal" organ of perverseness rather than a damaged organ of some other kind to account for destructive behavior. Also, as in "The Tell-Tale Heart" and "The Black Cat," the narrator aims less to account for his criminal actions than to make rational his irrational compulsion to expose them: phrenology becomes the science of inexplicable confessions.

The irony of this shifting of the "scientific" arguments of the insanity defense is even more significantly felt in the way it mirrors the radical alteration of moral perceptions Browne sought to effect for Singleton Mercer, that is, to convert his condemnable "*atrocious crimes*" to pitiable "*effects of disease.*" Such an alteration involves an excision of the moral content of ostensibly evil acts, a deflection of focus from the apparent value and meaning of the accused's actions—particularly their horrific aspect—to the physiological-psychological mechanisms that impelled them. Perhaps more than in either "The Tell-Tale Heart" or "The Black Cat," in "The Imp of the Perverse" the narrator is strikingly indifferent to the moral content or even the details of his crime. He does take some pride in his "deliberation" over "the means of the murder," but he trivializes the killing itself by devoting little space to it, describing the details as "impertinent" (p. 1224) and only hinting casually at a perfectly rational and culpable motive—greed. As in the insanity defense, what has redirected focus away from the killing and all but effaced its moral content has been a preoccupation with "*the prima mobilia* of the human soul*" (p. 1219). Put in terms of Poe's narrative strategy, a tale of greed and murder is reformed as an article on a quasi-scientific subject, the vitalizing human actions and motives approached so indirectly, the interest so redirected, as nearly to obliterate them altogether.

A final ironic turn on the insanity defense can be seen in the way Poe plays on the argument made by some critics of the defense that phrenology could be used to explain all criminal acts as the result of brain disease or injury. In the narrator's phrenology, perverseness is identified or proven not "*à priori*" by assumptions of God's mind or purposes, but "*à posteriori*" from an examination of "what man usually or occasionally did, and was always occasionally doing" (pp. 1219–20). Such an argument, of course, can be seen as a madman's fashioning universals out of his own insane proclivities. Nevertheless, the important point is that for Poe, as for the narrator, perverseness is clearly a propensity with a moral aspect or role. On the one hand, a "*mobile* without motive, a motive not *motivirt*," perverseness is a value-neutral "paradoxical something" that arises as the dialectically opposed concomitant of another principle or impulse. On the other hand, it is characterized as "an innate and primitive principle" to do ill or harm, the "overwhelming tendency to do wrong for the wrong's sake." He suggests that "we might, indeed, deem this perverseness a direct instigation of the archfiend, were it not occasionally known to operate in furtherance of good" (p. 1223). In this regard, one effect of the narrator's argument is to extend the range of phrenology to account for all acts, including all crimes, in terms of determined behavior.

But Poe's perverseness differs in operation from the theories of his narrators. That is, as set up or explained by the narrators in both "The Imp of the Perverse" and "The Black Cat," perverseness appears to be malign and destructive, but the stories' action demonstrates it to be ultimately beneficent and restorative. The effect seems comparable to the kind of justice achieved in such stories as "The Cask of Amontillado" (1846) and "Hop Frog" (1849), not a personal vendetta but a vengeance inherent in the Universe, "*graven . . . within the hills, and . . . upon the dust within the rock.*"[39] Considered as "*prima mobilia*" of the human soul—a constitutive feature of existence—perverseness seems to reflect the apocalyptic vision of Poe's *Eureka* in which the somethingness of existence predicates a prior nothingness, differentiation predicates a prior unity, and "*all* phaenomena [of existence] are referable to" the twinned principles of "'*attraction*' and '*repulsion*.'"[40] Such a vision, like the arguments underlying the concept of moral insanity, posits a universe that seems both deterministic and without clear moral order, one in which such stable categories as right and wrong, reason and unreason, are obliterated or, at least, blurred. But, for Poe, such a vision is at every point, in each side of every dialectic, a projection of God's will and ultimate purpose to return to the "normal" state of original Unity.[41] This indeed seems the case with perverseness, a principle of balancing negation inherent in the nature of existence, overriding will and antithetical to reason, a primary, indivisible determinant of human behavior whose effect is to address without motive or exterior purpose the horror of the trivialized murder, to secure, in other words, a form of justice through retribution.

At least in the three stories we have considered, Poe's centering of interest in "matters of psychology" can be understood not as indifference to moral issues but as a play on the treatment of those issues in the context of the insanity-defense controversy of his day. Whereas the insanity defense sought to alter radically the moral content of brutal acts, Poe's perverseness and the parallel confession compulsions in "The Tell-Tale Heart" and "The Black Cat" effect a radical restoration of their moral consequences. Both utilize a concept of obliterated will and "loss of the *use* of reason"—an aberration of normality in the insanity defense, a normality of aberration in Poe's perverseness. But, as if responding to the unsettling resolution of successful insanity defenses, the apparently incongruous disjunction between brutal acts and a response of pity or sympathy, Poe's deterministic forces lead the guilty to the hangman.

Chronology

1809   Born in Boston, January 19, as the second of three children of David Poe and his wife, Elizabeth Arnold, both actors. Poe's father abandoned the family.

1811   Death of Poe's mother, December 8, in Richmond, Virginia. The children are taken into diverse households, Edgar into that of John Allan, a Richmond merchant on December 26. Not legally adopted, he is nevertheless renamed Edgar Allan.

1815-1820   Resides with the Allans, first in Scotland, then in London.

1826   Enters the University of Virginia (founded by Jefferson the year before) where he studies languages. Gambling debts compel him to leave, after Allan refuses to pay them.

1827   Enlists in the United States Army as "Edgar Perry" in Boston where he publishes his first book *Tamerlane and Other Poems.*

1829   Frances Allan dies, February 28. "Edgar Perry" is honorably discharged as sergeant major and lives in Baltimore, where *Al Aaraaf, Tamerlane and Minor Poems* are published.

1830   Poe begins his academic studies at the United States Military Academy at West Point, New York.

1831	Expelled from West Point Poe lives in Baltimore with his father's sister, Maria Clemm, and her daughter Virginia, then eight years old. Begins to write tales. *Poems* is published in New York by Elam Bliss. William Henry Leonard Poe, Edgar's older brother dies in Baltimore.
1833	Poe receives prize for "MS Found in a Bottle" from a Baltimore publication.
1834	John Allan, Poe's foster father dies, March 27, in Richmond. Edgar's name is left out of the will.
1836	Poe moves to Richmond and becomes editor of the *Southern Literary Messenger.* Poe marries Virginia Clemm (aged 13) in Richmond.
1837	Poe leaves his position as editor and moves to New York.
1838	Poe moves to Philadelphia. *The Narrative of Arthur Gordon Pym* is published in New York by Harper & Brothers.
1839	Poe becomes editor of *Burton's Gentleman's Magazine* in Philadelphia.
1840	Publication of *Tales of the Grotesque and Arabesque* in Philadelphia.
1841	Poe becomes editor of *Graham's Magazine*, in which "The Murders in the Rue Morgue" is published in the April issue.
1842	Poe leaves his position at *Graham's Magazine.*
1843	"The Gold-Bug" receives $100 prize from the *Dollar Newspaper* in Philadelphia. *Prose Romances* is published in Philadelphia. Poe delivers his first lecture on American Poetry, also in Philadelphia.
1844	Poe moves to New York and works as editor on various publications.
1845	"The Raven" is published in the *New York Evening Mirror,* January 29. Poe's *Tales* and *The Raven and Other Poems* are published in New York by Wiley and Putnam.
1847	Virginia Clemm Poe dies of tuberculosis, January 30.

1848	The prose poem *Eureka* is published. Poe courts and becomes engaged to New England widow and poetess Mrs. Sarah Whitman. After Poe's failure to abstain from drinking, Mrs. Whitman breaks off her engagement.
1849	Poe begins a southern lecture tour and arrives in Richmond in July where he reunites and rekindles his youthful romance with Sarah Elmira Royster Shelton; they plan to marry.
1849	Poe dies in the Washington College Hospital in Baltimore on October 7. Rufus Wilmot Griswold publishes a slanderous obituary of Poe.
1850	Rufus Griswold publishes the *Works of the Late Edgar Allan Poe*, which includes a slanderous biography.
1860	Sarah Helen Whitman, Poe's former fiancée, publishes *Edgar Poe and His Critics*, a defense of Poe.
1874	John Henry Ingram puts out a new edition of Poe's collected works with a favorable memoir.
1875	The Poe Memorial is dedicated in Baltimore, November 17.
1910	Edgar Allan Poe is inducted into the Hall of Fame in New York.

Works by Edgar Allan Poe

A Dream (1827)

Dreams (1827)

A Dream Within a Dream (1827)

Evening Star (1827)

The Happiest Day, the Happiest
   Hour (1827)

The Lake. To – (1827)

Song (1827)

Spirits of the Dead (1827)

Stanzas (1827)

Tamerlane (1827)

Al Aaraaf (1829)

Fairy-Land (1829)

Romance (1829)

Sonnet—To Science (1829)

To ——- (1829)

To the River – (1829)

Alone (1830)

To – (1830)

To M— (1830)

The City in the Sea (1831)

Israfel (1831)

Lenore (1831)

The Sleeper (1831)

To Helen (1831)

The Valley of Unrest (1831)

The Coliseum (1833)

Manuscript Found in a Bottle (1833)

The Assignation (1834)

To One in Paradise (1834)

Berenice (1835)

Hymn (1835)

King Pest (1835)

Scenes from 'Politian' (1835)

To F— (1835)

To F—S S. O—D (1835)

Bridal Ballad (1837)

Silence—A Fable (1837)

Sonnet—To Zante (1837)

Ligeia (1838)

A Predicament (1838)

The Fall of the House of Usher (1839)

The Haunted Palace (1839)

William Wilson (1839)

The Man of the Crowd (1840)

Sonnet—Silence (1840)

A Descent into the Maelstrom (1841)

The Murders in the Rue
   Morgue (1841)

The Masque of the Red Death (1842)

The Pit and the Pendulum (1842)

The Black Cat (1843)

The Conqueror Worm (1843)

The Gold-Bug (1843)

The Tell-Tale Heart (1843)

Marginalia (1844)

Dreamland (1844)

Mesmeric Revelation (1844)

Eulalie (1845)

The Facts in the Case of M. Valdemar (1845)

The Purloined Letter (1845)

The Raven (1845)

The Cask of Amontillado (1846)

A Valentine (1846)

To M.L.S. (1847)

Ulalame (1847)

An Enigma (1848)

Eureka—A Prose Poem (1848)

To Helen (1848)

Annabel Lee (1849)

The Bells (1849)

Eldorado (1849)

For Annie (1849)

To My Mother (1849)

The Angel of the Odd—An Extravaganza (1850)

The Balloon-Hoax (1850)

Bon-Bon (1850)

The Business Man (1850)

The Colloquy of Monos And Una (1850)

The Conversation of Eiros And Charmion (1850)

Criticism (1850)

Diddling (1850)

The Domain of Arnheim (1850)

The Duc De L'Omlette (1850)

Eleonora (1850)

Elizabeth (1850)

Four Beasts In One—the Homo-Cameleopard (1850)

Hans Phaall (1850)

Hop-Frog or the Eight Chained Ourang-Outangs (1850)

How to Write a Blackwood Article (1850)

The Imp of the Perverse (1850)

The Island of the Fay (1850)

Landor's Cottage (1850)

The Landscape Garden (1850)

Lionizing (1850)

Literary Life of Thingum Bob, Esq. (1850)

Loss of Breath (1850)

The Man That Was Used Up (1850)

Mellonta Tauta (1850)

Metzengerstein (1850)

Morella (1850)

Morning on the Wissahiccon (1850)

The Mystery of Marie Roget (1850)

Mystification (1850)

The Narrative of Arthur Gordon Pym of Nantucket (1850)

Never Bet the Devil Your Head (1850)

The Oblong Box (1850)

The Oval Portrait (1850)

The Power of Words (1850)

The Premature Burial (1850)

Serenade (1850)

Shadow—A Parable (1850)

Some Words With a Mummy (1850)

The Spectacles (1850)

The Sphinx (1850)

The System of Dr. Tarr And Prof. Fether (1850)

Tale of Jerusalem (1850)

A Tale of the Ragged Mountains (1850)

The Thousand-And-Second Tale of Scheherazade (1850)

Thou Art the Man (1850)

Three Sundays in a Week (1850)

Von Kempelen and His Discovery (1850)

Why the Little Frenchman Wears His Hand in a Sling (1850)

X-ing a Paragrab (1850)

The Devil In the Belfry (1839)

Imitation (1827)

Works about Edgar Allan Poe

Canny, James R. and Charles F. Heartman, *A Bibliography of the First Printings of the Writings of Edgar Allan Poe*; Hattiesburg, Miss.: The Book Farm, 1943. (Reprinted, Millwood, New York: Kraus Reprint Co.)

Carlson, Eric W., ed., *A Companion to Poe Studies*, Westport, Connecticut: Greenwood Press, 1996.

Dameron, J. Lasley and Irby B. Cauthen, Jr., *Edgar Allan Poe: A Bibliography of Criticism, 1827–1967*; Charlottesville: University Press of Virginia (for The Bibliographical Society of the University of Virginia), 1974.

Deas, Michael J., *The Portraits and Daguerreotypes of Edgar Allan Poe*; Charlottesville: University Press of Virginia, 1989.

Foye, Raymond. Ed. *Edgar Allan Poe The Unknown Poe*. San Francisco: 1980.

Honer, Stanley M., *Invitation to Philosophy: Issues and Options*, New York: Wadsworth Publishing Company, 1996.

Lee, Robert A., *Poe's Tales: The Art of the Impossible. The Nineteenth—century American Short Story*, New Jersey: Vision Press Limited, 1985.

Mabbott, Thomas Ollive, ed, *The Collected Works of Edgar Allan Poe*; (Vols. 1 –*Poems*, Vols. 2 & 3–*Tales and Sketches*) Cambridge, Mass.: The Belknap Press of Harvard University Press, Vol. 1–1969 (Second printing 1979), Vols. 2–3–1978 (Second printing 1979).

May, Charles L., Edgar Allan Poe: *A Study of the Short Fiction*, Boston: Twayne Publishers, 1991.

Muller, John P. and William J. Richardson, *The Purloined Poe: Lacan, Derrida, and Psychoanalytic Reading*. Baltimore: Johns Hopkins University Press, 1993.

Poe Studies, Pullman, Washington 99164-5910: Washington State University Press, Cooper Publications Building, Washington State University. Vols. 1–30. (1967–1997).

Quinn, A. Hobson, *Edgar Allan Poe: A Critical Biography*; New York: D. Appleton-Century, 1941 (Reprinted–New York: Cooper Square, 1969 and again, Baltimore: Johns Hopkins University Press, 1998.

Silverman, Kenneth, Edgar A. Poe: *Mournful and Never-ending Remembrance*; New York, 1991.

————, ed. *New Essays on Poe's Major Tales*. Cambridge University Press, 1993.

Thomas, Dwight and David K. Jackson, *The Poe Log: A Documentary Life of Edgar Allan Poe, 1809–1849*; Boston: G.K. Hall & Co.

Thompson, G. Richard, ed., *Essays and Reviews*, New York: The Library of America, 1984.

Wagenknecht, Edward Charles. *Edgar Allan Poe, The Man Behind the Legend*. New York: Oxford University Press, 1963.

Walsh, John Evangelist. *Midnight Dreary: The Mysterious Death of Edgar Allan Poe*. New Brunswick, NJ: Rutgers University Press, 1998.

Contributors

HAROLD BLOOM is Sterling Professor of the Humanities at Yale University and Henry W. and Albert A. Berg Professor of English at the New York University Graduate School. He is the author of over 20 books, including *Shelly's Mythmaking* (1959), *The Visionary Company* (1961), *Blake's Apocalypse* (1963), *Yeats* (1970), *A Map of Misreading* (1975), *Kabbalah and Criticism* (1975), *Agon: Toward a Theory of Revisionism* (1982), *The American Religion* (1992), *The Western Canon* (1994), and *Omens of Millennium: The Gnosis of Angels, Dreams, and Resurrection* (1996). *The Anxiety of Influence* (1973) sets forth Professor Bloom's provocative theory of the literary relationships between the great writers and their predecessors. His most recent books include *Shakespeare: The Invention of the Human*, a 1998 National Book Award finalist, and *How to Read and Why*, which was published in 2000. In 1999, Professor Bloom received the prestigious American Academy of Arts and Letters Gold Medal for Criticism.

KAY CORNELIUS is a former English teacher who lives in Huntsville, Alabama. She frequently writes about history. Her interest in Edgar Allan Poe began when she started reading Poe's stories in middle school. *Edgar Allan Poe* is her fourth book published by Chelsea House.

COURTNEY J. RUFFNER and **JEFF GRIENEISEN** are doctoral candidates at the University of South Florida. Courtney teaches English and British Literature and directs the Foreign Language Laboratory at Manatee Community College where Jeff also teaches English. Both teach at the Writing Studio at the Ringling School of Art and Design, and together they coedit a graduate and faculty creative writing journal titled *The Red Raven Review*.

JOHN CLEMAN received his Ph.D. from the University of Wisconsin and teaches American literature and American studies at California State University, Los Angeles. He is the author of "Irresistible Impulses: Edgar Allan Poe and the Insanity Defense," which was published in *American Literature*.

Notes

IRRESISTIBLE IMPULSES: EDGAR ALLAN POE
AND THE INSANITY DEFENSE

1. *Edgar Poe: Seer and Craftsman* (Deland, Fla.: Everett/Edwards, 1972), p. 181.

2. "The Poetic Principle," *Edgar Allan Poe: Essays and Reviews*, ed. G. R. Thompson (New York: Library of America, 1984), p. 78.

3. Rev. of *Twice-Told Tales* by Nathaniel Hawthorne, Thompson, p. 576.

4. *Poe: A Critical Study* (Cambridge: Harvard Univ. Press, 1957), pp. 190, 194.

5. Davidson, p. 194.

6. *Edgar Allan Poe* (New Haven: College and University Press, 1961). p. 72.

7. Citations for "The Tell-Tale Heart," "The Black Cat," and "The Imp of the Perverse" will be to *Tales and Sketches, 1843–1849*, ed. Thomas Ollive Mabbott, Vol. 3 of *Collected Works of Edgar Allan Poe* (Cambridge: Harvard Univ. Press, 1974) and will be included within the text.

8. See Roger Smith, "The Boundary Between Insanity and Criminal Responsibility in Nineteenth-Century England," in *Madhouses, Mad-Doctors, and Madmen: The Social History of Psychiatry in the Victorian Era*, ed. Andrew Scull (Philadelphia: Univ. of Pennsylvania Press, 1981), p. 365.

9. See Thomas Maeder, *Crime and Madness: The Origins and Evolution of the Insanity Defense* (New York: Harper and Row, 1985). The trials referred to are those of James Hadfield (1800), John Bellingham (1812), and Edward Oxford (1840). In the McNaughton case, the accused had bungled an attempt to assassinate the Prime Minister, Robert Peel, shooting instead Peel's private secretary. The event occurred during the period of the Chartist uprisings and was thought by some to be part of a political conspiracy. McNaughton's acquittal so outraged the British, public that the House of Lords was directed to devise guidelines in determining culpable insanity in order to prevent such acquittals in the future. These guidelines are known and still cited as the "McNaughton Rules."

10. Michel Foucault, *Madness and Civilization: A History of Insanity in the Age of Reason*, trans. Richard Howard (1961; New York: Vintage-Random, 1988). See especially chap. 2, "The Great Confinement," pp. 38–64.

11. Poe satirizes these reforms in "The System of Doctor Tarr and Professor Fether."

12. See Levine; Elizabeth Phillips, "Mere Household Events: The Metaphysics of Mania," *Edgar Allan Poe: An American Imagination* (Port Washington, N.Y.: Kennikat, 1979), pp. 97–137; and Allan Smith, "The Psychological Context of Three Tales by Poe," *Journal of American Studies*, 7(1973), 279–92.

13. "By the Southern Mail: The Trail of Singleton Mercer for the Murder of Hutchinson Heberton," *New York Herald*, 29 March 1843, p. 2.

14. Charles S. Brigham in his edition of *Edgar Allan Poe's Contributions to "Alexander's Weekly Messenger"* (Worcester, Mass.: American Antiquarian Soc., 1943) describes this report of Wood's trial as "Distinctly by Poe" (p. 64). see also Mabbott, p. 798.

15. Joseph Jackson, "George Lippard: Misunderstood Man of Letters," *Pennsylvania Magazine of History and Biography*, 59 (1935), 383.

16. A special "Double Number" supplement of the Philadelphia *Dollar Newspaper* devoted entirely to the Mercer trial was issued on 4 April 1843, the day before the regular edition of the same weekly announced the short-story prize-contest to which Poe submitted "The Gold Bug."

17. See David S. Reynolds, *George Lippard* (Boston: Twayne, 1982), pp. 10–11.

18. Justifiable homicide was actually the first point of defense, insanity the second, but the judge's instructions to the jury virtually negated the

argument that the murder was justified ("Trial of Singleton Mercer," *Public Ledger*, 7 April 1843, p. 2).

19. In America, the Mercer case caused more of a sensation than did the McNaughton trial, but the two were frequently linked as symptomatic of a decline in law and order. For example, in the view of one contributor to the *New York Herald*, "The trials and acquittals of McNaughton, Mercer, and [Alexander] McKenzie, are all pregnant illustrations of the same general fact—the growing and alarming laxity in the administration of criminal justice" ("Administration of Criminal Justice," 19 April 1843, p. 2). See also "Licentiousness and Crime," *New-York Daily Tribune*, 13 April 1843, p. 2; "Criminal Justice" by An Old-Fashioned Fellow, Letter, *New York Herald*, 15 April 1843, p. 2; and "Murder Made Honorable," *Public Ledger*, 18 May 1843, p. 2.

20. Maeder, p. 7.

21. Browne quotes Justice Tracy from the trial of Edward ("Mad Ned") Arnold in 1724. See Maeder, pp. 10–11.

22. "Trial of Singleton Mercer," *Public Ledger*, 31 March 1843, p. 2.

23. *A Treatise on The Medical Jurisprudence of Insanity*, ed. Winfred Overholser (Cambridge: Harvard Univ., Press, 1962), p. 43.

24. Ray, p. 169.

25. S. P. Fullinwider, "Insanity as the Loss of Self: The Moral Insanity Controversy Revisited," *Bulletin of the Institute of the History of Medicine*, 49 (spring 1975), 94.

26. John Starett Hughes, *In the Law's Darkness: Isaac Ray and the Medical Jurisprudence of Insanity in Nineteenth-Century America* (New York: Oceana, 1986), pp. 18–19.

27. "Trial of Singleton Mercer," *Public Ledger*, 31 March 1843, p. 1.

28. Reports of the trial of Benjamin White in January 1843—shortly after the first publication of "The Tell-Tale Heart"—offer striking parallels to Poe's tale. In court White admitted killing his father, rejected the arguments of insanity that had been the basis of his lawyer's defense, and insisted on the rationality of his motives and actions, but he became clearly agitated and irrational while recounting his feelings about the victim. ("A Wi[lful?] Murder of a Father by his own Son—the Effects of Infidelity and Irreligion," *New York Herald*, 4 April 1843, p. 1).

29. "Trial of Singleton Mercer," *Public Ledger*, 31 March 1843, p. 1.

30. Phillips, pp. 128–30.

31. Ray, p. 110.

32. Ray, p. 170.

33. Brigham, pp. 63, 64.

34. Brigham, p. 63.

35. Brigham, p. 64. Poe's language here closely parallels that of the summation of the trial in the *Public Ledger* ("The Case of Wood," 30 March 1840, p. 2).

36. J. Gerald Kennedy, *Poe, Death and the Life of Writing* (New Haven: Yale Univ. Press, 1987), pp. 134–35.

37. Phillips, pp. 131–36.

38. In the discussion of perverseness after the sentence, "Of this spirit philosophy takes no account," the earliest published version of "The Black Cat" includes the line, "Phrenology finds no place for it among its organs" (Mabbott, p. 852).

39. *The Narrative of Arthur Gordon Pym, in Edgar Allan Poe: Poetry and Tales* ed. Patrick F. Quinn (New York: Library of America, 1984). p. 1182.

40. "Eureka: A Prose Poem," Thompson, p. 1282.

41. Joseph Moldenhauer argues similarly in linking Poe's moral and aesthetic visions with the cosmology of *Eureka* ("Murder as a Fine Art: Basic Connections between Poe's Aesthetics, Psychology, and Moral Vision," *PMLA*, 83, [1968], 284–97).

Index